GEORGE MEREDITH AND THOMAS LOVE PEACOCK: A STUDY IN LITERARY INFLUENCE

A THESIS

IN ENGLISH

PRESENTED TO THE FACULTY OF THE GRADUATE SCHOOL OF THE
UNIVERSITY OF PENNSYLVANIA IN PARTIAL FULFILLMENT
OF THE REQUIREMENTS FOR THE DEGREE
OF DOCTOR OF PHILOSOPHY

AUGUSTUS HENRY ABLE, 3RD.

ERRATA

Page 7, line 5. For 'wish' read 'wishing'

Page 35, line 15. For 'follows' read 'follow'

Page 37, lines 6–7. For 'Shagpat' read *Shagpat*

Page 104, line 9. For 'groups' read 'group'

PHILADELPHIA
1933

To
R. V. L. A.
AND
A. H. A.

TABLE OF CONTENTS

PAGE

I
Introduction.. 7

II
Prentice Work.. 16

III
An Aspect of the Comic Spirit................................. 37

IV
Of Sentimentalism and Its Cure................................ 46

V
The Spectacle of England...................................... 56

VI
The Dinner Table and Afterward............................... 75

VII
Woman... 88

VIII
Sources and Types of Characterization: Friends, Notorieties, and Eccentrics.. 102

IX
The Discovery of the Celt..................................... 117

X
A Point of Style.. 129

ACKNOWLEDGMENT

The author wishes to acknowledge his indebtedness to Professor Cornelius Weygandt of the English Department of the University of Pennsylvania, at whose suggestion this thesis was undertaken and by whose help and counsel it proceeded. Dr. Allan Chester and Dr. Robert Sechler, of the same department, for their most friendly office of reading the proof, are also to be thanked; as are likewise the authorities of the University Library for their courtesy in making ready the necessary books.

I
INTRODUCTION

George Meredith was a genius of literature, an original spirit who troubled his contemporaries both by the challenge of his ideas and the willful eccentricity of his style. Moreover, he was a man of proud nature, willing to shoulder the burden of his uniqueness, one little wish to acknowledge debts to anyone in his own generation or before him. That Meredith, however, no matter how little confessing, felt the impress of others, cannot be doubted, since even genius cannot work in a void, exempt from the influence of its age, and the influences of particular individuals and examples. Indeed the privilege of genius seems to lie most, not in its freedom from the contacts and forces that mould lesser men so noticeably, but in its power to assimilate that which is round about it and to achieve thereby new syntheses. For example, the sources of Chaucer lie abroad where they may be espied by the curious in such things; and Shakepeare's method of appropriation is sufficiently notorious to be regarded as a commonplace of his history. The discovery then of his sources is held, quite justly, no derogation to the artist; for the principle of *ex nihilo nihil* is understood to operate in the craft of letters no less than in any other art; than in the mechanic trades, or, indeed, in any act of life. Rather, do we marvel at his power of transmutation, his skill in giving new meaning and color to old things. So it is that George Meredith is interesting as an object of study. Aloof from his contemporaries, imperfectly understood except by his faithful circle of intimates, conceding nothing to public taste, and acknowledging no debts, he appears isolated in his age. Accordingly, the common assumption in regard to him of a lack of literary debtorship, which is wide of the facts. Rather, the truth is that Meredith's title to fame, like the titles of the other "greats" of English letters, lies grounded in no simple originality, but in his power of transcending others; since he, too, was an adaptor of ideas and an imitator in various modes of story telling. To ideas he gave a new freshness, winging them aloft until they became inescapable in the sight of men; in the more formal technique of literature he was less uniformly successful, sometimes rising above his models, sometimes falling short of them. His successes are the enduring basis of his reputation; his comparative failures in experimentation, of little moment since he is not to be judged by them. The important fact is that he was, like others, pupil and apprentice in his time.

Meredith's masters in his apprentice period were many, and the best.[1] We find him at school to Dickens, following in many places that novelist's methods in characterization and incident.[2] The Cogglesly brothers of *Evan Harrington*, for example, are an obvious copy of the Cheerybyles out of *Nicholas Nickleby*. In the same manner, the earlier life of Harry Richmond is evidently written with the type of *David Copperfield* in mind. Characters like Captain Welsh, the Christian skipper, in *Harry Richmond*, and little Skepsey, the pugilistic clerk of *One of Our Conquerors*, are pure Dickens. Again, Thackeray, though in less degree than Dickens, plays his part as tried model for Meredith. Richmond Roy surely finds his prototype in Thackeray's genial rogue, Barry Lyndon. And it must be added that both the characters of Old Mel and the female adventuress, the ever memorable Countess de Saldar, in *Evan Harrington*, in their hinted pretensions exhibit traits of Thackeray's same arch-charlatan. George Eliot, too, it seems, must be written into the list of Meredith's creditors, for *Rhoda Fleming*, besides certain easily discernible Dickensean elements, shows, in its motif of sisterly devotion and the stern promptings of duty, a parallel both in theme and scene to her work. Of all her books it suggests most pointedly *The Mill on the Floss*, published just five years previously. Among the non-fictional writers of the day in England, Carlyle, of course, bulks largest as an influence on Meredith;[3] both in philosophy and turns of style, the reverberations from that source are numerous and distinct.

---

[1] Bailey, E. J., *The Novels of George Meredith: A Study*, New York, 1907, Ch. III, pp. 45–99.
[2] Priestley, J. B., *George Meredith*, New York, 1926, in *English Men of Letters*, Ch. VII, p. 175.
[3] Moffatt, J., *George Meredith, A Primer to the Novels*, London, 1909, pp. 9–10.

Of these contemporaries, however, with the exception of Carlyle, the influence is fleeting. Thackeray and George Eliot are lost from the scene early; and Dickens becomes only an occasional echo. Morover, Meredith by his later rating down of Dickens has given evidence that his taste finally turned away from that author who was once his study.[4] But another great formative influence on Meredith, not hitherto mentioned in the list, yet remains, an influence under which he essayed his first work in fiction, an influence of continuing potency whose mark is shown even to the last in *Celt and Saxon;* namely, that of Thomas Love Peacock, one time his father-in-law.

The period of Meredith's actual association with Peacock was comparatively brief, less than a decade. However, it was sufficiently long to establish an intellectual *rapprochement* between the two that, so far as its influence on the younger man was concerned, was never to be lost. In the years between his marriage to Mary Ellen Peacock (Mrs. Nicolls) in 1849 and her leaving him in 1858, Meredith lived almost constantly, except for the time spent on excursions to the sea-side, in proximity to Peacock, first at Weybridge, later at Lower Halliford just across the common from Peacock's home.[5] In 1853 he was actually a resident of Peacock's house and it was there that his son, Arthur Gryffyth Meredith, was born. During all this period Peacock seems to have shown a most kindly interest in the young couple. He brought them out of lodgings into his own home when they were needy, and later established them in their own cottage nearby.[6] Moreover, it is believed that it was through the good offices of Peacock, who was himself a contributor, that Meredith got his entry into the pages of *Frazier's Magazine*, and had his *Poems* printed by J. W. Parker & Son, the publishers of *Frazier's*.[7]

---

[4] Ellis, S. M., *George Meredith, His Life and Friends in Relation to His Work*, London, 1902, Ch. IV, p. 81. George Meredith, *Letters, Collected and Edited by His Son*, New York, 1912, Vol. I, p. 290.
[5] Priestley, J. B., *Thomas Love Peacock*, New York, 1927, in *English Men of Letters*, Ch. IV, p. 82.
[6] Ellis, S. M., *George Meredith, His Life and Friends in Relation to His Work*, London, 1920, Ch. IV, p. 78.
[7] Seccombe, Thomas, *George Meredith*, in *Dictionary of National Biography*, Supplement II, p. 606.

Internal evidences of a very cogent sort, too, would seem to indicate that Peacock actually aided in the writing of Mary Meredith's essay *Gastronomy and Civilization* for *Frazier's*, in which, it is generally believed, Meredith also had a hand. That Peacock's kindliness was not thrown away on Meredith is amply demonstrated by his dedication of the *Poems* (1851) to Peacock "in affection and respect." However, with the debacle of his marriage, Meredith's friendship with Peacock must suddenly have ceased. There are no letters extant that refer to Peacock; not even in conversation with his intimate friends would Meredith discuss the relation.[9] Indeed, it would seem that Meredith even destroyed all available copies of his *Poems* in order that their dedication to Peacock might be forgotten.[10] Accordingly, in subsequent years practically all record of their fellowship was lost, since Meredith himself chose to bury it out of sight; and, on the other hand, the biographers of Peacock relied chiefly for their data on the information of Mrs. Clarke, the daughter of Mary Meredith by her first husband, Lieutenant Nicolls, who never alluded to Meredith at all in connection with her grandfather.[11]

From Meredith's acquaintance, however, the importance of his early relation with Peacock was not entirely lost sight of. Evidently, in spite of Meredith's consistent effort to avoid it, in the play of conversation the subject would occasionally crop out; and in his work the influence of his father-in-law did not escape notice. Lady Butcher, in her *Memories of George Meredith*,[12] after remarking upon the dedication of the *Poems* to Peacock, writes most significantly: "He used to declare it was a great advantage to him in his youth to have been associated with Peacock, and that Peacock's writing had been a great model for him." This bit of evidence is full of meaning as giving an

---

[8] Freeman, A. M., *Thomas Love Peacock*, London, 1911, Ch. IX, pp. 318–320. Ellis, S. M., *George Meredith, His Life and Friends in Relation to His Work*, London, 1920, Ch. III, pp. 62–65.
[9] Priestley, J. B., *George Meredith*, New York, 1920, in *English Men of Letters*, Ch. I, p. 15.
[10] Hardman, Sir William, *A Modern Pepys*, edited by S. M. Ellis, London, 1923, p. 87.
[11] Young, A. B., *The Life and Novels of Thomas Love Peacock*, 1904, pp. 17–18.
[12] Butcher, Lady Alice, *Memories of George Meredith*, London, 1919, p. 92.

historical substantiation to the obvious truth, so often cited but so little studied, with which Lady Butcher concludes: "It is quite easy in comparing the novels of Mr. Meredith with those of his father-in-law to trace the influence that helped form his style. . . ." This is the same observation that was made many years ago by James Thomson in his reviews of *Richard Feverel* and *The Egoist*—"He has the quaint fantastical humor of the poet and scholar and thinker—freakish touches of Sterne and Jean Paul and Carlyle and his own father-in-law (Peacock of *Nightmare Abbey*, *Gryll Grange*, *Headlong Hall*, and other enjoyable sojourning places, who had Shelley for a friend.)[13] Or again, concerning the Rev. Mr. Middleton, he writes: ". . . he is of the family of Drs. Folliott and Opimian, with whom you have excellent converse in the *Crotchet Castle* and *Gryll Grange* of the humorous and caustic Thomas Love Peacock."[14] One further scrap of information from Edward Clodd is interesting as throwing light upon the intimate *causeries* in which Meredith and Peacock must often have indulged.[15] "Keats," he quotes Meredith as saying, "is a greater poet than Shelley; in this Peacock agreed." And then Meredith continues to tell how he had been unable to press the claims of Tennyson on Peacock. Such are the paltry fragments in which Meredith's personal friends have touched upon his one-time relationship with Peacock. In the way of salvage they are little; but they are most significant for what they say, pointing to Meredith's recognition of a debt so far as he ever owned it, and, not less important, to his contemporaries knowledge of it.

Mrs. Sturge Gretton, who was close to Meredith in his later years, has also written on the topic.[16] It is she who inplies that it was the stabilizing influence of Peacock's character that kept the inevitable break between Meredith and his wife from coming earlier than it did. That a personal relationship existed between Peacock and Meredith, apart from the paternal kindness of

---

[13] Thomson, James, *Cope's Tobacco Plant*, Vol. 11, No. 110, May, 1879.
[14] Thomson, James, *Cope's Tobacco Plant*, Vol. 11, No. 110, January, 1880.
[15] Clodd, Edward, *George Meredith, Some Recollections*, *Fortnightly Review*, July, 1909, pp. 24–25.
[16] Gretton, Mary Sturge, *The Writings and Life of George Meredith*, London, 1926, pp. 17–18.

the elder man, is unquestioned, in spite of the evidence of temperamental incompatibility. The two men constantly met as neighbors and members of the same family; and for a time were forced together as the inmates of a single dwelling (even though it was divided in two); and in Peacock's pleasant living room overlooking the river, Meredith must, often and long, have listened to Peacock's wisdom, and, lounging, read his books.[17] And Peacock, lover of the classics, arm-chair philosopher, man of letters, and experienced student of affairs, had much to give. Consequently, his influence was of no narrow strain. It was as wide as his speculations, which related not only to the theory of literature, but beyond that to the problems of society and the central questions of wise living. That Meredith, young, poor, and imperfectly educated, should have listened with respect to the opinions of Peacock, almost seventy years of age, well-to-do, experienced in the ways of men and books, is little surprising. The marvel would have been if he had done otherwise.

Accordingly, almost all the biographers and critics who have written of Meredith have commented, briefly at least, upon the influence of Peacock on him. The debt of Meredith in that direction is almost universally acknowledged; and, although the degree of affirmation varies, the opinion is so well established as to have the prestige of a generally recognized truth. The matter, however, has been but imperfectly investigated; never really sifted. Many have contented themselves with blanket statements concerning an influence, general in scope, "on thought and style."[18] A few, more investigative, have pointed out specific details of influence—sometimes in a way most illuminating and creditable to their scholarly interest.[19]

---

[17] Galland, René, *George Meredith Les Cinquante Premières Années*, Paris, 1923, pp. 79–88.

[18] Morley, Viscount John, *Recollections*, London, 1917, Book I, Ch. IV, p. 37. Young, A. B., *The Life and Novels of Thomas Love Peacock*, London, 1904, p. 18. Seccombe, Thomas, George Meredith in *Dictionary of National Biography*, Supplement II, p. 606.

[19] Moffatt, James, *George Meredith, A Primer to the Novels*, London, 1909, p. 8. Chislett, William, Jr., *Notes and Queries*, Vol. 10, p. 208. Chislett, William, Jr., *George Meredith, A Study and Appraisal*, New York, 1926, p. 145. Gretton, Mary S., *The Writings and Life of George Meredith*, London, 1926, p. 606.

Others, less informed, have ventured half-commitments on the subject, as if reluctant to declare themselves absolutely on an ambiguous, unproved point.[20] On the other hand, the minimizers of the influence, the dissenters from the established view of its existence are few, and these would seem to be such from a fear of glibness, an unwillingness to join too readily in the chorus of opinion.[21]

Behind the often repeated generality, however, there does lie a very real truth, one of incomparably larger dimension and significance than has ever been claimed. The fact is, the influence of Peacock on Meredith's work is both formative and permeative. In things both great and small, it shows itself through practically the whole line of Meredith's books. It is rock in the foundations of his philosophy, whether it be of the Comic Spirit, or emancipated woman, or of man as a political animal. It appears in his picturing of society, its recreations and foibles, its false emotions and false values. It sets out the dinner table, and regales the company with good wine and good talk. It gives characters and incidents and scenes to the story. It points, at times, the diction itself of our novelist. Moreover, besides showing itself in so many facets of Meredith's work, it is, as has been stated farther back, an enduring influence. In Meredith's earliest fiction *The Shaving of Shagpat* and *Farina*, it shows baldly in all sorts of ways, not only in the spirit of the narrative, but in its subject matter and its embellishment. With Meredith's abandonment of the fantastic, romantic tale of adventure, however, it does not disappear; it merely takes on new form. With the emergence of Meredith's social comedy, it manifests itself in a less directly imitative manner; rather than in turns of style, it is present in the underlying *motifs* of thought, the philosophical approach of the author to his material, although surface appear-

---

[20] Photiades, Constantin, *George Meredith, His Life, Genius, and Teaching*, translated by A. Price, London, 1913, p. 37. Frey, Eugen, *Die Romane George Meredith's: Ein Versuch*, Winterthur, 1913, p. 5.

[21] Elton, Oliver, *Modern Studies*, London, 1917, Vol. II, *Mr. George Meredith*, p. 23. Van Doren, Carl, *The Life of Thomas Love Peacock*, New York, 1911, pp. 265–66.

ances of it still are not lacking. Only for a brief period, is it really lost sight of. In *Rhoda Fleming* (1865) and *Vittoria* (1866) it vanishes. But it is only for the time. *Harry Richmond* again shows traces of it; and *Beauchamp's Career* is full of remembrances. From then on, the influence is again easily traceable. And with the years, rather than diminishing, it increases; until, at the very close of his period, Meredith's work betrays the lingering strain of Peacock, in characterization and incident, as fully as at any earlier time. That Meredith's study of his one-time father-in-law's work outlived the severance of the family tie is proved conclusively by the echoes in his pages of *Gryll Grange*, Peacock's last novel, of 1861. Accordingly, the whole body of Meredith's work ties up to the whole corpus of Peacock's writing. His admiration of the elder man's work was strong enough to survive the bitterness of domestic tragedy, and to draw him continually to his work for a model and the inspiration of ideas. On a proud nature like Meredith's no influence could levy a greater tribute.

In advancement of this claim of Peacock's influence, it must be admitted that the approach to the whole subject must be almost exclusively through the study of such internal evidences, in the way of resemblances and the parallelisms of ideas, as the books themselves of the respective authors afford. Because of the lack of direct evidence there is no other practicable method of investigation; and because the life of Meredith has been pretty fairly reviewed now, and no new clues bearing on the subject brought to light, the likelihood of there ever being any other seems fairly slight. Accordingly, the method of comparison recommends itself because of its availability. In defense of this method of study, Mr. George Saintsbury, in a wise paragraph, writing of the sources of Thomas Love Peacock, says:[22] "Nothing comes of nothing; and though there is absolutely no more foolish and useless style of criticism than that which would fain make out that somebody copied somebody else, there is none more sage and more fruitful than that which endeavours to find out

---

[22] Saintsbury, George, Introductions to *Maid Marion* and *Crotchet Castle* by Thomas Love Peacock, London, 1895, p. IX.

what somebody had in his mind, consciously or unconsciously, when he wrote something." Further, he writes: "the main interest of the juxta-position of them [authors] is that it supplies one more of those literary filiations which are the most interesting things in literary study."

It is with the thought that these words embody that this study of Meredith and Peacock is undertaken. The words 'juxta-position' and 'filiation' are most fitting. They represent perfectly the nature of that effort that should be made in bringing together the works of Thomas Love Peacock, too little appreciated for his genuine values of thought, hitherto regarded chiefly as a skeptical and self-contradictory humorist; and the works of his greater son-in-law, George Meredith. The literary influence that flowed from one to the other, as we have seen, is generally admitted. But a complete and detailed study to present fully the evidence of their literary relationship has never been made. Accordingly, this attempt is made to bring the works of Peacock and of Meredith into juxta-position, in order that they may be compared for resemblances, not, it is hoped, such general ones as may be merely fortuitous, the parallel workings of two minds that, no matter how different, must necessarily, even in this multiform and many-visioned world, sometimes strike things alike; but for those that may show a genuine kinship born of common experience and ideas. So, perhaps, a literary filiation may be worked out; illustrating a relation, not of copier and copied, of plunderer and plundered, which never existed, but one demonstrating the transcription and transmutation of thoughts as they passed from one mind to the other in the natural way of memory and of appreciation. That some such "son-ship" did exist between Peacock and Meredith seems not only warrantable in theory but provable by text.

II

'PRENTICE WORK

The Shaving of Shagpat

Of all Meredith's books *The Shaving of Shagpat* would seem the most likely to show traces of the influence of Peacock. Such an expectation may be justified upon two grounds: first, the fact that *Shagpat* is Meredith's first fiction, and, as a beginning, likely therefore to show, more or less, that imitation, that feeling after a model, to which fledgling writers are prone; secondly, because the time of its creation coincides with the period of Meredith's residence near, or, as for a time, actually in the house of his father-in-law, whom we know he admired and who might serve as a literary mentor. Apparently the work was begun in 1852, while the Merediths were in lodgings at Weybridge, an evil time for them "with duns at the door." Then in 1853 Peacock, compassionating the poor couple, took the Merediths into his own house at Lower Halliford. And there the book was carried forward. It was completed, however, at Vine Cottage on the other side of Halliford Common, whither shortly the Merediths removed, since crotchety Peacock and nervous Meredith had failed to prove mutually agreeable.[1]

Between the two men then during this period of close residence, we can predicate, with some assurance, an exchange of ideas, a rather heavy traffic in them, as may be judged from the evidence of Meredith's later novels.[2] And certainly it seems there must have been also the reading of books out of Peacock's library. Books of all sorts must have been borrowed by Meredith: classics, Italian romances, Welsh bardic poetry; and, not least of all, Peacock's own novels. This influence that came to Meredith from Peacock's books can not be lightly dismissed. It is second in value only to the impression which Peacock, the man himself, made

---

[1] Ellis, S. M., *George Meredith*, London, 1920, pp. 76–78.
[2] For the best account of this period of residence, see René Gallan's *Les Cinquane Premières Anneés*, Paris, 1923, pp. 79–88.

upon Meredith by the exposition of his ideas and theories. That Meredith knew Peacock's novels intimately the whole range of his own work reveals. But beyond this, his literary references in many quarters show a remarkable coincidence with those of Peacock. That Meredith should have so many references in common with his father-in-law, and conversely, so few apart from him, can logically be explained in only one way—the reliance of them both on the same books, that is, Peacock's collection of books. These books, whether of his own writing, or his mere possessing, are an integral part of Peacock's influence on Meredith.[3]

The most successful of Peacock's books, according to the standard of popular success, was *Maid Marian*, that romantic satire-burlesque on Robin Hood and his merry men which Peacock had published back in 1822.[4] And, as companion piece to it, there was the even more delicious, though less popular, *The Misfortunes of Elphin* (1830), constructed most artfully from the legends of ancient Wales. These were Peacock's most successful stories; but what was perhaps more interesting about them to a prospective author: they were not only saleable, they were of a type, as it must have seemed to Meredith, comparatively easy to write; stories of high adventure, of large free action, stories, in short, of a kind easy "to string". Then too, Meredith, from his German school days must have been familiar with stories of the kind.[5] It happens that there is a passage in *The Adventures of Harry Richmond* that seems to throw light in that very direction.[6] Harry and his friend Temple, it may be remembered, are on one occasion lost in the depths of the German forest with night coming down. To them it seems like a haunted place; certainly it is one calculated to arouse memories of fearsome stories. It is

---

[3] In addition to the integration of Meredith's and Peacock's Welsh references to which attention is given later (Chapter IX), mention must also be made of their common allusions to the Italian poets, particularly Boiardo and Berni. Mr. James Moffatt (*Primer*, p. 283) has called attention particularly to a most interesting parallel in their use of a certain incident from Boiardo's *Orlando Inamorata*.
[4] Saintsbury, George, Introduction to *Maid Marian* and *Crotchet Castle*, London, 1895, p. XV, p. XXVII.
[5] Selincourt, R. E., *The Life of George Meredith*, New York, 1929, p. 13.
[6] *The Adventures of Harry Richmond*, Vol. 9, Ch. XV, p. 176.

with this suggestion of the scene that Temple remarks on the "upsetting" nature of German folk legends. Whereupon Harry Richmond, in a spirit of fiendish glee and with a genius of invention, immediately improvises a brief burlesque of the romantic story of horror upon a variation of the Faust theme. Harry, who momentarily hypnotizes his companion with his story, in commenting upon it calls it 'absurd'. That Meredith, here, is writing with an eye upon himself is seemingly confirmed by the testimony of Mrs. Ross (Janet Duff-Gordon) and Lady Butcher, who tell that he used to delight them and his other younger acquaintance around Weybridge by improvising just such yarns.[7] The love of the extravagant which was in his nature found vent in these offerings to a juvenile, unsophisticated audience. It is not surprising then that he should attempt to practice in the same way, albeit in a more elaborate, artistic form, upon his elder public. In fact, we know that part of *Shagpat*, the Bhanavar episode, came into existence in just that way.[8] So, in regard to the genesis of his first two stories as wholes, it may be assumed that Meredith, familiar with the genre of the mediaeval romantic story, found it not only simple as a model of composition but delicious as a subject for playful, bantering treatment; exactly the sort of theme that allowed to the author all sorts of play for satire and the expression of exuberant high spirits. And if Meredith found the form congenial, he also remembered that Peacock had used it, with the most considerable success he had enjoyed. *Maid Marian* had even won its way to the footlights, being produced as an operetta. In view then of these considerations of personal taste and profitable example, it is not surprising that Meredith chose to begin his career with a book like *Shagpat*.

At first sight the position of *Shagpat* may seem rather anomalous. It has elements that suggest debts of relationship in several places. Perhaps its nearest relation in English letters seems to be Beckford's *Vathek*, a book with which it has some obvious

---

[7] Ellis, S. M., *George Meredith*, London, 1920, p. 62. *Letters*, Vol. 28, I, p. 12. Butcher, Lady Alice, *Memories of George Meredith*, New York, 1919, p. 10.
[8] Ellis, S. M., *George Meredith*, London, 1920, p. 84.

features in common.⁹ The three chambers, for example, in the Palace of Aklis, are reminiscent of the Palaces of the Senses which the Caleph of Bagdad had built for his enjoyment. Vathek had a palace dedicated to each sense; in Meredith this series is telescoped, and the material is developed a bit differently in accordance with the moral purpose of the author. In the first chamber of Aklis, Shagpat faced the temptation of wealth. There, where fountains of gems played continually, men with the heads of beasts wallowed in a flood of riches. The second chamber of Shagpat's temptation was the place of gluttony, where beasts with the heads of men gorged themselves without ceasing upon food and drink, and sniffed rarest perfumes. The third chamber was the house of the women: where Shagpat temporarily succumbed to the temptresses' wiles. All these features are clearly suggestive of *Vathek*, yet the treatment is sufficiently different to attest Meredith's originality.

Of the allegorical element in *Shagpat* which would indicate a far-off filiation for it with *Bunyan's Pilgrim's Progress*, it is perhaps best to say little, especially as in no case can the allegory affect the narrative elements as such. Prof. John Mackechnie has given us a key to the many meanings of the story, and has secured Meredith's approval for his interpretation, as is attested by a commendatory letter of Meredith's published as a foreword[10] to his book. This certification, of course, does not agree very well with the disclaimer of any didactic purpose that Meredith introduced into the second and third editions of 1855 and 1872 respectively;[11] and agrees only partially with the letter that Meredith wrote to Mrs. Bovril in answer to her inquiry concerning the allegory of *Shagpat*.[12] "Shagpat", writes Meredith, "I suppose does wear a sort of allegory. But it is not a dress suit; rather as a sort of dressing gown, worn very loosely. And *they say* it signifies Humbug and its attractiveness; while Noorna is the spiritual truth, poor Shibli Bagarag being the ball between the two.

---

[9] *Cf. Vathek*, Ch. I, with *The Shaving of Shagpat*, Vol. I, pp. 200–205.
[10] Mackechnie, John, *George Meredith's Allegory, The Shaving of Shagpat, Interpreted*, London, 1905.
[11] Hammerton, J. A., *George Meredith, His Life and Art in Anecdote and Criticism*, Edinburgh, 1911, p. 10.
[12] *Letters*, Vol. 29, II, p. 459.

I think I once knew more about them and the meaning but have forgotten and am glad to forget." This uncertainty in Meredith's mind concerning his allegory: his denial of it and later his partial, and finally full admission of it, are hard to understand. But the piece gives the sense of allegory. The ordinary reader is conscious of it, I think, as he reads; he feels that the involved, and often confused, adventures have their significance, that they are not mere happenings, the flashings of a brilliant imagination, but that each has a meaning to which he finds it difficult and not quite worth the trouble to penetrate, especially so as the story itself is so good. As an allegory it is simply one of that line of books in English, reaching down from *Piers the Plowman*, through *The Faerie Queen*, and *Pilgrim's Progress*, that bear a message beneath their more manifest artistry.

Of the story of *The Shaving of Shagpat* itself, George Eliot in her favorable notice in the *Westminister Review*, called it "a thousand and second Arabian night." In writing for *The Leader* an earlier review in January of the same year, she had praised the fiction for its originality. "It has none of the tameness which belongs to mere imitations manufactured with servile effort, or thrown off with simious facility. It is no patchwork of borrowed incidents."[13] And this opinion, as George Eliot also pointed out, was the one which Meredith himself wished to establish when he wrote the author's prefatory note, stating that the work was no translation, that it came from no Eastern source, but was in every respect an original work. His desire was to imitate the manner and spirit of the Arabian story-tellers, but the materials were entirely his own.

From what sources then were these materials derived? *The Story of Bhanavar, the Beautiful* has been accounted for by Mrs. Ross (Janet Duff-Gordon), who tells how Meredith got the basic idea for that episode from a traveller's tale told by a M. de Hauxthausen whom Meredith met at the Gordon's house,

---

[13] Eliot, George, *Westminster Review*, April, 1856, quoted in full by Hammerton, *George Meredith*, pp. 141–42; *The Leader*, January, 1856, reprinted in *Some Early Appreciatives of George Meredith*, edited by M. B. Forman, New York, 1909.

Nutfield Cottage, Weybridge.[14] M. de Hauxthausen "had fought with the Queen of Serpents, whose crown he wore in a little red silk bag that hung around his neck from a gold chain." The fight had been a hard one, for the Queen in desperation had called her subject serpents to her aid; and they had come. But the adventurous de Hauxthausen had killed the Queen despite all and had carried off her crown, a bony excresence of the head, that he kept with him always. Meredith, according to Mrs. Ross' account, as recounted by Ellis, was fascinated by the recital of the stranger, and shortly afterward, on a homeward walk, told to her, the little girl of whom he was so fond, a story derived from it. Such then was the chance origin of the Bhanavar episode, perhaps the most beautiful part of the Shagpat cycle, which is a frame to it.

The Story of Bhanavar the Beautiful, however, constitutes roughly only a third or less of the tale of Shagpat, so that the greater part of the story must be accounted for, after Bhanavar is dismissed. The general source of the main story, I believe, is to be found in Peacock's long narrative poem, *Rhododaphne*, published in 1818, a poem much admired at the time, which had won favor not only with the indiscriminating, but the praise of Shelley and of Byron in England, and of Poe in America,[25] Of this most pretentious of Peacock's poetical efforts, J. B. Priestley has written, very justly, I think:[16] "It is not surprising that *Rhododaphne* has been praised so widely and by such good judges. It is not surprising simply because the poem has solid merits and is, indeed, an excellent specimen of its kind. To begin with, it is a narrative poem that has a genuine narrative . . . Again it is one of the few poems dealing with the ancient classical world that really seem animated by the spirit of that world. In reading it we do not feel that we are attending a masquerade. We may not feel that we are actually living in that world—but we at least feel that we are looking at it from afar."

Rhododaphne is a tale of Thessalian magic, similar in kind to

---

[14] Ellis, S. M., *George Meredith*, London, 1920, p. 84.
[15] Priestley, J. B., *Thomas Love Peacock*, New York, 1929, in *English Men of Letters*, p. 38.
[16] *Ibid.*, p. 118.

those found in Apuleius and Petronius. It is interesting that Peacock after writing Rhododaphne did not revert to such a theme again until the very close of his career. In *Gryll Grange* (1861) the guests while away one winter evening in telling horrific tales of witchery, most of them retold from the aforementioned Latin sources.[17] The recurrence is interesting, because it is unique. Peacock after writing *Rhododaphne* abandoned the theme of magic; his interests lay elsewhere. His knowledge of it came naturally in the course of his classical reading; he saw the possibilities of it for romantic fiction, and used it. But then it became buried away, lost to sight, an unimportant curiosity to be resurrected only on a very dull evening at the Grange when wits were low.

That Meredith should have known *Rhododaphne*, however, is not not strange. If Meredith, as indeed Edward Clodd, tell us,[18] tried in vain to make Peacock appreciate Tennyson, it is quite likely that Peacock tried to advance his own poetical theories and favorites with his son-in-law. Moreover, both Meredith and Peacock were poets. Meredith was a beginner in the art; Peacock a retired practitioner. And if Peacock's name was not great, certainly his reputation was creditable. He was a minor poet of the old school. Surely his chief and best work could not escape Meredith's attention. And as Mr. Priestley has said, *Rhododaphne* does tell a good story.

Because Meredith took various hints from *Rhododaphne*, which he freely mingled in the narrative of *Shagpat*, it may be well to set forth the argument here, briefly.

Anthemion, a youth of Ladon, comes to the festival of Love at Thespia, to make offerings for the recovery from a wasting sickness of his beloved, Calliroë. Standing before the statues of Love (there are three of these: The Creative, The Heavenly or Uranian, and The Earthly or Pandemian), he is distressed to see the Uranian Venus frown upon him, while the Pandemian goddess smiles wickedly. He is distressed, too, to see his "wild-flower" wreath wilt in his hands. Sick at these portents, he is recalled to himself by a girl of more than

---

[17] *Cf. Gryll Grange*, Ch. XXXIV, pp. 270–77.
[18] Clodd, Edward, *George Meredith: Some Recollections, Fortnightly Review*, July, 1909, pp. 24–25.

human beauty, asking what ails him. Seeing the loss of his flowers, she offers him some of her own, urging him to a second sacrifice. Timidly he takes half of her flowers and places them on the altar. These, however, do not fade; this offering is apparently acceptable. Then Anthemion's companion throws down her flowers; whereupon quite miraculously the two offerings fall together and cling in a single mass. The girl, well pleased, gives Anthemion a flower, making him promise to wear it in her remembrance, until it shall fade. Reluctantly the youth promises; then hastens off among the joyous throng of worshippers.

Wandering alone, distraught, among the crowd, Anthemion is accosted by an old man who asks him why he, at the festival of Love, wears "the laurel-rose, to Love profane." "Beware," says this stranger. Anthemion then relates his story, and the old man tells him of the laurel-rose that there is "no herb or plant of deadlier might" in magic. Anthemion, worried, seeks advice. The old man tells him at sun-down to call on his Natal Genius, at the same time casting over his shoulder, into a stream, the bewitching flower; but under no circumstances is he to look back while he is doing this. Anthemion follows instructions and hears, as the flower falls into the water, the voice of Calliroë, his betrothed. Forgetting all else, Anthemion turns about; but sees nothing unusual, only the stream flowing by, untroubled. Later, wandering through the Grove of the Muses, Anthemion meets his acquaintance of the altar. She enchants Anthemion now by her singing, and reproaches him for casting away her flower. She laughs at his expression of fear; she tells her name: Rhododaphne. Moreover she tells how an oracle prophesied their meeting in all its minutest circumstances, as it had befallen that day. In short, she claims him for her own. She kisses him, saying,

> "These lips are mine,
> Poison to all lips but mine."

After this, Anthemion, quite distracted, decides to return home; accordingly, he flees away.

Anthemion, upon his return, finds Calliroë fully restored. She flies to greet him. In the evening, while they sit in affectionate embrace, Anthemion kisses Calliroë. Immediately she grows pale and expires in his arms. Then the youth remembers the words of Rhododaphne. Distracted utterly, Anthemion now rushes away; he knows not whither.

Wandering on the sea-shore, Anthemion is spied by a pirate craft, and taken prisoner. Shortly afterward, other pirates returned from roving, bring on board booty, including a young woman of rare beauty. It is Rhododaphne, of course. The seamen presently ask the girl to sing; she accommodates them, but sings songs not to their liking, since she sings of wreck and their loss. That same night a storm arises. The boat founders with seeming death to all aboard, except Anthemion, whom the girl carries in her arms to safety.

Once on shore, however, Anthemion begins to rebuke Rhododaphne, as the cause of all his woe. He asks in despair, "What would'st thou with me, fatal maid?" In answer she claims his love. Whereupon Anthemion pleads that his love is dead; that he can love no more. To which speech Rhododaphne replies:

> "The Genii of the earth, and sea,
> And air, and fire, my mandates hear."

She hints at her power to renew love or life itself, if she call on Daemogorgon. Rhododaphne, however, will not compel Anthemion's love. She is going, she says, to retreat into a cottage and there she will await him, if he cares to come.

Continuing his lonely journey, Anthemion comes to a temple; he enters and surveys the place. He is in a room of many columns, with statues of demons and of kings, "throned in order round," "with seeming life". One brazen image sits alone, "a dwarfish shape, of wrinkled brow". Suddenly, at the sound of Anthemion's tread, "that image rose and spake, 'What would'st thou?'" Anthemion, much shaken by this wonder, asks food and rest for the night. To this request the image courteously replies:

> "Enter! fear not: thou art free
> To my best hospitality."

Accordingly, Anthemion passes into a room of great beauty, fitted with every luxury, where a sumptuous feast is spread. There he eats and drinks, served by "a golden boy." He hears music, the singing of maidens. Then a ravishing beauty appears; it is Rhododaphne. "Now thou art mine!" again she cries.

So lovely is Rhododaphne in her new appearance that Anthemion's eyes swim with dizziness. The lamps grow dim. He loses all sense of time and place. So he enters upon a new life with Rhododaphne in her enchanted palace. However, in spite of all her blandishments, Anthemion cannot quite forget the past. He is haunted continually in the midst of entertainment by a familiar face. It is the face of Calliroë which haunts him, nor can all the endeavor of Rhododaphne "from his constant memory sever the image of that dearer maid."

The power of Rhododaphne is at this point described. We are told that the daemons of earth are slaves to her. One night, however, Rhododaphne finds herself deserted by her attendants; she calls for them, but they do not come. The dwarf-monarch of the outer hall has disappeared from his place, and there throned in his stead is the likeness of Uranian Love. Immediately this Love draws her bow and shoots an arrow (borrowed from Apollo) at Rhododaphne. She falls, pierced through, and dies instantly. At the same moment the great palace falls asunder and Anthemion, who cannot but grieve for Rhododaphne, finds himself in his familiar Thessalian dale. Calliroë's cottage is nearby, whence from the door she comes forth in bloom of health, radiantly restored. Her spell has been broken by the death of the enchantress. So there is happy reunion, and to the story a pleasant close.

If the tale of *Rhododaphne* has been presented in rather detailed fashion, it is only in order that the points of resemblance between it and *Shagpat* may be the more clearly enforced. For, indeed, there are similarities, both of a general and of a particular sort. In the first place, both stories deal in magic—the magic of human transformations, and both involve the fortunes of a poor young man who is quite unexpectedly dragged, willy-nilly, into the web of magical formulae. Such comparisons, general and tenuous, would of course be worth little if they stopped there. In the case of *Shagpat*, however, a closer examination only serves to establish, in further particulars, scarcely accidental parallels with the theme of *Rhododaphne*.

The situation, for example, in *Shagpat* of Noorna and the enchantress Goorelka, matches surprisingly the fundamental relation between Calliroë and Rhododaphne. Rhododaphne had power over the life of Calliroë through the agency of a laurel-rose; Goorelka, the wicked princess of Oolb, practiced on Noorna, transforming her into a hag, by means of the Lily of the Enchanted Sea. And, similarly, in both instances, the spell was broken: for Calliroë, by a supernatural intervention; for Noorma by Shibli Bagarag, the Barber, who uprooted the Lily of the Sea. In both instances the formula is exactly the same: it is the story of one woman temporarily, by black art, appropriating the life of another, exchanging place with her. Noorna, the daughter of the Vizier, Feshnavat, was transformed into a hideous crone by Goorelka, Princess of Oolb. The punishment of Goorelka is, in her turn, with the failure of her spell, to become a creature of identically the same sort; and Noorna, released from bondage, assumes the identical beauty of the glorious Goorelka; so that her espoused barber does not know her, thinking her the wicked princess. The situation here is exactly parallel to that of Rhododaphne. With Calliroë's renewal of life, Rhododaphne must herself die. It is in both stories as if two women shared between them one life, one beauty, which passes from one to the other, and back again. Such is the basic formula in both cases, a clear and obvious one, but sufficiently peculiar and distinctive to preclude the chance of mere accidental resemblance.[19]

In the same way, between the temptation *motifs* of both stories a nice parallel may be drawn. Meredith, however, has associated the temptation episode of Shagpat with a second temptress, the Queen Rabesqurat. In this he differs from the simpler treatment of Peacock, who creates but one character, Rhododaphne, sorceress. The episodes then that in Peacock are all associated with one character are in Meredith assigned to two: Goorelka, of whom we have already spoken, and Rabesqurat.

Concerning Rabesqurat and her palace there are several things worthy of notice. In the first place, one of the first persons, next the Queen herself, whom Shibli Bagarag saw there, was the dwarf, Abarak, "a little man, humped, with legs like bows, and arms reaching to his feet". This creature, who strangely resembles the bonze of Rhododaphne's hall, was the superintending deity of Rabesqurat's palace. It is remarkable, too, that he, like his ugly counterpart of Peacock's story, finally deserts his mistress, thereby bringing down catastrophe on the Queen.

Another noteworthy resemblance to Peacock's narrative is found in the scene where Shibli, having fainted, on return to consciousness finds himself in a pleasant garden place, fitted, however, much like a room with rich upholsteries and lamps.[20] There, clad in silk robes, he reclines at ease and enjoys music. All this is very suggestive of the reception of Anthemion in the house of Rhododaphne. Presently there comes a maiden who leads him off to where the Queen Rabesqurat is. The greeting of the Queen, although less possessive than that of Rhododaphne to Anthemion, is, nevertheless, much the same in spirit. "O youth, my husband, to whom I am a bride," she says, claiming him.

The situation which follows, however, is even more positively reminiscent of *Rhododaphne*. Meredith has developed, at length, with insight and with humor, the confusion of mind that was

---

[19] *Cf. The Shaving of Shagpat*, Vol. I, p. 158; *Rhododaphne*, Cant. VII, p. 253.
[20] *Cf. The Shaving of Shagpat*, Vol. I, p. 182; *Rhododaphne*, Cant. VI, p. 222.

Shibli's under the surprising circumstances of his seduction. Just as Anthemion was haunted by a vague reminiscence of the past, so is Shibli.

When the Queen asserted her betrothal with him, Bagarag marveled saying, "This is a game, for indeed I am no husband, neither have I a bride . . . yet I have a confused memory of some betrothal . . ."

"Thereupon she cried, 'Said I not so? And I the betrothed?'"

"Still he exclaimed 'I cannot think it!'"

"Now he was wiled by the enchantments of the Queen, caught in the snare of her beguilings, and he sat there awhile in the midst of feastings, mazed, thinking: What life have I lived before this, if the matter be as I behold?"[21]

At last, perplexed to know which might be his real life, the haunting past or the dreaming present, Shibli begins to ask Rabesqurat questions, desiring to know "Is there truly now such a one as Shagpat in the world?" or again, "And one, daughter of a Vizier?" The answer being unsatisfactory, Shibli might have remained in lasting perplexity if the sudden, bitter memory of his "thwackings" had not convinced him of the reality of the past and freed him from the spell.

The shrewd Bagarag, freeing himself by sharp questions and self-analysis, is a very different person from poor Anthemion, who may scarce be said to have any character at all. He, witless youth, is the victim of circumstance merely. But the situation of the two is alike, and their perplexity the same. A comparison of the two must lead to the conclusion that Meredith in his writing was influenced undoubtedly by a memory of the other. The situation is a delicate one, dealing as it does with the intangibilities of mind. Traced out too realistically it might become horrible; too imaginatively, merely fantastic. Peacock had escaped both these extremes by being merely factual and pedestrian. In Meredith the treatment is radically different. Meredith keeps all the physical trappings of Peacock's story; in fact, enlarges upon them so that everything is lifted to the utmost physical splendor. His Queen Rabesqurat is redoubtable in her

---

[21] *Cf. The Shaving of Shagpat*, Vol. I, p. 184; *Rhododaphne*, Canto VII, p. 234.

glory; one feels the menace of her palace and of herself, because, as it were, he has seen them. In the same way, Meredith takes the character of the hero, makes him less attractive physically, but endows him with wit and all sorts of Oriental cleverness, so that he is no longer a mere victim, but a protagonist in his awful conflict with infernal powers. Moreover, Meredith introduces the element of a sly humor in Bagarag's questions to lighten the situation and make it more sympathetic to the reason. In all these things there is an elaboration, an enrichment of the basic theme, although in its outline it is one with Peacock's original.

In one last episode of *The Shaving of Shagpat* the resemblance is so close to one of Peacock that the parallel is indubitable. This incident, as like the other incidents of *Rhododaphne* which he appropriated, Meredith has taken bodily from its position in the original narrative and fitted to an entirely new set of events. This, as we have seen, he did in two other instances. The present reference is to the chamber of buried kings in the Palace of Aklis. Shibli Bagarag, having yielded there to the temptation of being crowned king by the maidens of the palace, finds himself presently imprisoned in a small dark cell, buried alive. It is not our business to reveal here how Shibli freed himself from his cell. The point is: he was not alone in his plight. The following passage describing the situation may well be collated with a passage from *Rhododaphne*, in the Sixth Canto.[22]

Shagpat	*Rhododaphne*
And the throne as he sat on it moved out of the chamber into the hall . . . and on every side the hall's doors opened, and he marvelled to see men, young and old, beardless and venerable, sitting upon thrones, crowned with crowns, motionless, with eyes like stones in their recesses.	The daemons of the earth that know The beds of gems and fountain springs Of undiscovered gold and where In subterranean sepulchres The memory of whom place doth bear No vestige, long-forgotten kings Sit gaunt on monumental thrones With massy pearls and costly stones Hanging on their half-mouldered bones, Were slaves to her.

---

[22] *Cf. The Shaving of Shagpat*, Vol. I, p. 207; *Rhododaphne*, Canto VII, p. 254.

It would seem that in the lines from *Rhododaphne* quoted above, we have first in the reference to "beds of gems" and fountain-springs of gold, the genesis of those fountains of jewels, before mentioned, that Shibli passed by safely in the outer court of Aklis, prior to his imprisonment. The parallel of the place of buried kings, a striking image, with Meredith's hall of sleeping kings, is most sure.

Another interesting resemblance between *Shagpat* and another of Peacock's books, *The Misfortunes of Elphin*, is to be found in the persistent and rather strained use of a rhetorical device, a kind of trope, intended for humorous effect, that Peacock himself had used most successfully. The figure would seem basically to be related to the form of the Welsh Triad, at least Peacock uses it first in such a way as to suggest its affiliation with that gnomic form.[23] In Chapter I of *The Misfortunes*, telling of the royal pursuits of Gwythno, King of Gwaelod, he says:[24] "The chase conduced to the good cheer of the feast, and to the good appetite which consumed it; the cheer inspired the song; and the song gladdened the feast and celebrated the chase."

Here then are described three good things, all of which bear a mutual and supporting relation to each other. Shortly afterward we find this same figure taking on the more extended and common form, a debased variety of the original, tighter form. Describing the office and duties of Seithenyn,[25] Lord High Commissioner of the Royal Embankment, Peacock writes: ". . . he (Seithenyn) executed it as a personage so denominated might be expected to do: he drank the profits, and left the embankment to his deputies, who left it to their assistants, who left it to itself."

Whence, from such source, springs a passage like the following in Meredith's *Shagpat* (the porter Ukleet is telling Bhanavar the Beautiful of her repute in the palace and how it came to be): "There was always babbling of thy case, O my princess, till the head-cook seized hold of it, and so it went to the chamberlain, thence to the chief of the eunuchs, and from him in a natural

---

[23] Saintsbury, George, Introduction to *The Misfortunes of Elphin*, p. IX.
[24] *The Misfortunes of Elphin*, p. 4.
[25] *The Misfortunes of Elphin*, p. 5.

course to the King. Now from the King the tracking of the tale went to the under-cook down again, and from him to me."

Toward the end of *Shagpat* this figure becomes expanded to inordinate length. Describing the agitated gossip that passed in the streets of Oolb in the portentious minutes just before the shaving of Shagpat, Meredith writes (I abstract the passage, for it would be superfluous to quote it all):[26] ". . . Now from Krooz il Krazowik, the carrier, they went to Dob, the confectioner; to Azawol, the builder; and from Azawol, the builder, to Toheik, the collector of taxes; and each referred to some other."

This figure like the one before quoted is double-returning, in that the information having passed through a circuit of persons to a destination, returns again through them to its source. So is the original character of the Peacockian trope preserved, although on a tremendously extended scale.

If this borrowing of the stylistic figure is allowed, as I think it must be, it, added to the other evidences already mentioned, argues that Meredith used Peacock's works, very definitely, not only as a mine of material, but as a stylistic model. This fact, of course, derogates in no way from the worth of Meredith's performance. Certainly in his use of the sources of *Rhododaphne* he improves upon all he touches. Meredith's style, too, is altogether his own: indeed, it is only where he attempts to follow Peacock's style that measurably he fails. Surely the verse of *Shagpat*, interpolated after the fashion of Peacock, is undistinguished; and the one special figure of Peacock's that he employs, as I have just shown, tends to be overblown. The fact, very simply, is that Meredith, as a 'prentice hand, was feeling his way, adapting, improvising; taking hints and suggestions from various sources, but turning them in his own unmistakable original way. The influences, as we have seen, appear in theme, in scene, in incident, in character, and in style. But he was not writing from any one model; he was simply suggestible to influence, and most abundantly, as to the freshest, nearest, most constant source of influence upon him in those days, to that of Thomas Love Peacock.

---

[26] *The Shaving of Shagpat*, Vol. I, pp. 272–73; also p. 67.

Farina

When in 1857 Meredith wrote his burlesque-romance, *Farina, A Legend of the Rhine*, he was still working in that imitative period that had produced *Shagpat*. In a general sense and in several of the particulars, *Farina* suggests Peacock's *Maid Marian;* in its spirit it is very close to that story. The spirit of *Shagpat*, of course, had been that of the Arabian Nights, although, as we have seen, its elements were garnered elsewhere. But *Farina* in its feeling approaches nearer than anything else Meredith ever wrote to the spirit of Peacock. The plot of the story, however, it must be admitted, is drawn very largely from a contemporary source: namely, Charles Kingsley's novel, *Westward Ho*, that had appeared just the year before its writing (1856). Noticing the time of composition, we may assume that Meredith determined upon his burlesque immediately upon reading Kingsley's story. In it he must have seen good game; and justly so, for Kingsley's biased, chromo-colored picture of Elizabethan England, with its ultra-sentimental, romantic core, must have drawn laughter from the great satirist-to-be of the sentimental and the false.

In general outline the two stories, *Farina* and *Westward Ho* (so far as it concerns the fortunes of Rose Salterne, the Rose of Torridge, and her Noble Brotherhood of the Rose) tally almost exactly, except that the former has a happy close, in the traditional style. Margharita, like her sister of *Westward Ho*, was a blonde, most fair, whom to look on was to love. Her father was Gottlieb Groschen, a merchant prince, one of the great burgers of Cologne. In this worthy we have a likeness to Rose's father, the mayor of Bideford (then one of the great ports of England) and a merchant of large wealth. In both instances, too, the young men of the neighborhood act in a remarkably similar manner to show their devotion to the common idol, for she is no less, of their hearts. In Cologne the young men not only organize to protect Margharita, but joust and duel continually in her honor. They call themselves the Company of the White Rose. In England, with characteristic British reserve and orderliness, the swains organize merely to protect Rose from annoyance, and to keep the peace. The German heroine is abducted by a robber baron of the Rhine, Werner by name. In like manner, though less forcibly, Rose Salterne is carried away by Don Guzman de Soto, a wicked Spaniard, who has been held temporarily for ransom at Bideford. Margharita, more fortunate than Rose, is carried, however, only to an inaccessible castle some miles up her native river; while the unfortunate Rose is carried across the Atlantic to grace the governor's house at La Quayra, in the Spanish Indies. In both cases expeditions of rescue are made by the knightly bands of sworn protectors. The German band is successful, probably because they have the good fortune to be abetted by an Englishman, The Goshawk, who with his lone staff for weapon, strangely suggests a leaner, more agile Friar Tuck; while the English company are defeated by the unwillingness of Rose herself and the machinations of another Englishman, her real betrayer. So far do the stories run in remarkable parallel. In some respects, the English story is more absurd than its burlesque, for the fitting out of the good ship Rose and enrollment of volunteers is more pretentious, far, and incredible, than the expeditionary force sent against Werner's Eck.

So much for the debt to Kingsley, the inspirer of the burlesque and chief contributor to the theme. That Meredith should have chosen the Rhineland as his setting is not at all remarkable. His choice of it was probably dictated by the same circumstances that led Peacock to choose a Welsh subject in writing *The Misfortunes of Elphin:* namely, a love of the countryside about which he wrote and a considerable knowledge of its antiquities. Meredith had brought home to England, from his school-days at Neuwied, a love of the Rhine, among whose hills he had tramped and, undoubtedly, a fund of those legends in which that country is so rich.[27]. Moreover, although Meredith's admiration for the Germans is undoubted, it is altogether likely that he early saw in certain of their traits matter for laughter, even as Peacock did in the Welsh. The physical grossness of much of their life, their eating, and drinking, their capability of a stolid animal contentment—characteristics contrasting so strangely with their quixotic enthusiasm and loyalties, their

[27] Selincourt, R. E., *The Life of George Meredith*, New York, 1929, pp. 11–12.

naïveté as expressed in their charming, yet often frightful legends—must even in his school-days have impressed Meredith's discerning spirit.[28] So it is that, in accordance with his later expressed ideal of the Comic Spirit, he can and does write of these people of contradictions satirically, caring for them all the while.

In spite of the fact that Meredith chose to make *Farina* a burlesque on Kingsley's current novel, and to use the familiar scenery of the Rhineland as his locale, the book, as has been stated before, is written in the spirit of Peacock, with both the *Misfortunes of Elphin* and *Maid Marian* as models. This shows forth in abundant details, such, for example, as the quotations from the Minnesingers, whose wisdom is quoted in the same way as is that of the bards in *The Misfortunes of Elphin*. Sentences from Heinrich von der Jungferweide and Hans Aepfelmann of Duesseldorf give that gnomic touch which Peacock supplies from the Triads, or from the poetry of Aneurin, Taliesin, or old Llywarch. The resemblance of the Goshawk to Friar Tuck of *Maid Marian* has already been pointed out. Armed only with his staff, this character turns up opportunely, as was the habit of the earlier hedge priest, to help in dangerous adventure. The boisterous comedy, too, is reminiscent of Peacock. The panic fits of the puritanical Aunt Lisbeth are in point. Her speech, too, has a Peacockian ring on occasion, as in that delightful instance when out of her own mouth she confounds her innocence. Speaking of Margharita, she says: "I believe she knows as much as I do . . . Such are girls nowadays. When I was young— oh! for a maiden to know anything then—oh! it was general reprobation. No one thought of confessing it.[29]" Such a turn of humor is true Peacock. Of the heroine it may be said that she, too, is a true Peacockian heroine: a physically strong, alert girl, frank and unrestrained in her joy of life, yet modest and decorous. There is also in the insistence on appetite as a sign of health and its gratification as a good, an echo of one of Peacock's most persistent *motifs*. "Prove", says Gottlieb to the

---

[28] *The Adventures of Harry Richmond*, Vol. 9, Ch. XIV, pp. 173–174.
[29] *Farina, A Legend of the Rhine*, Vol. 21, p. 56.

Goshawk, "you are a true hero by your appetite—for everywhere the badge of subjection is a poor stomach."[30] It is the remark of the typical Peacockian host.

The final and most cogent proof of the relationship of *Farina* to the romantic narratives of Peacock, however, can be found in more specific citations than any yet offered. A comparison of the opening of *The Misfortunes of Elphin* with that of *Farina* is especially noteworthy as showing resemblance. If one collates the opening sentences of the two works, he is struck by a perfect parallelism, the evident copying by Meredith of an exact formula. Allowing for the change of names and countries, the items in series are all alike. But let the passages themselves exhibit the likeness.[31]

Misfortunes of Elphin	*Farina*
In the beginning of the sixth century	In those lusty ages
when Uther Pendragon held the nominal sovereignty of Britain over a number of petty kings	when the Kaiser lifted high the goblet of Aachen, and drank elbow upward, the green-eyed wine of old romance
Gwythno Garanher was king of Caredigion	there lived, a bow-shot from the bones of the ten-thousand virgins and the three Holy Kings, a prosperous Rhinelander, by name Gottlieb Groschen . . .
The most valuable portion of his dominions was the great plain of Gwaelod . . . This district was populous and highly cultivated. It contained sixteen fortified towns, superior to all the towns and cities of the Cymry, except Lleon upon Usk;	Wine hills, among the hottest sun-bibbers of the Rheingau glistened in the rôle of Gottlieb's possessions; corn-acres below Cologne; basalt-quarries above Linz; mineral-springs in Nassau—
And like Lleon they bore in their architecture, their language, and their manners, vestiges of past intercourse with the Roman lords of the world	A legacy of the Romans to the genius and enterprise of the first German traders

Here in the two introductions we see a parallel carried down through a series of four successive steps. First, in each case, the

---

[30] *Ibid.*, p. 182.
[31] Cf. *Farina, A Legend of the Rhine*, Vol. 21, p. 4; *The Misfortunes of Elphin*, p. 3.

age is identified by its ruler; then follows the name and office of the principal of the story itself; then an account by inventory of his possessions, and finally a reference to the antiquity of the country, mention in both cases being made of the Romans, who as "lords of the world" had left traces in places as widely separated as Germany and Wales. Of the two descriptions, as is usual, Meredith's is the more picturesque, because of his use of concrete imagery, but in both the formula is carried out exactly.

Nor is this the only instance where there is a close parallelism in *Farina* to a feature of Peacock's narrative. Equally noteworthy perhaps with the introduction in this respect, is one lyric, a hunting-song, sung by the members of the White Rose Club and introduced in the midst of the narrative, which reproduces in spirit a song of Peacock's Friar Tuck in *Maid Marian*. The two songs follows.[32]

Farina	*Maid Marian*
The Kaiser went a-hunting, a-hunting, tra-ra:	Though I be now a grey, grey friar,
With his high horn at springing morn,	Yet I was once a hale young knight;
The Kaiser trampled bud and thorn! Tra-ra!	The cry of my dogs was the only choir In which my spirit did take delight.
And the dew shakes green as the horsemen rear,	Little I recked of matin bell
And a thousand feathers they flutter with fear;	And drowned its toll with my clanging horn;
And a pang drives quick to the heart of the deer;	And the only beads I loved to tell, Were the beads of dew on the spangled thorn.
For the Kaiser's out a-hunting! Tra-ra!	
Ta, ta, ta, ta, Tra-ra, Tra-ra, Ta-ta, Tra-ra, Tra-ra!	

---

[32] *Cf. Farina, A Legend of the Rhine*, Vol. 21, pp. 46–47; *The Misfortune of Elphin*, p. 30.

The wild boar lay a-grunting,
   A-grunting, tra-ra!
And, boom, comes the Kaiser to hunt up me?
Or, queak! the small birdie that hops on the tree? Tra-ra!
O birdie, and boar, and deer, lie tame,
For a maiden in bloom, or a full-blown dame,
Are the daintiest prey, and the windingest game,
When Kaisers go a-hunting, Tra-ra!
Ha, ha, ha, ha,
   Tra-ra, Tra-ra,
Ha-ha, Tra-ra, Tra-ra!
	An archer keen I was withal,
	And ever did lean on green-wood tree;
	And could make the fattest roebuck fall,
	A good three hundred yards from me.
	
	Though changeful time with hands severe,
	Has made me now those joys forego,
	Yet my heart bounds whene'er I hear
	Yoicks! hard away! and tally ho!

It is interesting that in both instances the song is sung in the presence of the heroine, although the more demure German maid does not join, like her heartier English cousin, in the rounding out of the chorus. The two songs in their narrative elements are not alike; Peacock's is personal with his friar, and elegaic in note, as are most of Peacock's best lyrics; whereas Meredith's is merely recitative. But many of the details are alike: the reference to the horn, and the deer, and the thumping chorus, so characteristic of the glee. Peacock, always a lover of the open and of Old English ways, which in his day he saw threatened and fading before the "march of progress," could write such a glee with genuine feeling. And so too could Meredith, who was of sympathetic temper with Peacock in regard to the out-of-doors, and old ways and customs. It is significant that he makes the English Goshawk, listening, finally join in the chorus, and then exclaim, "That's a trick we're not half alive to at home." One can be sure that Meredith appreciated Peacock's charming song; he imitated it well. It is the borrowing of such special features of Peacock's work that makes the imitative element in *Farina* especially interesting. Meredith there shows a decidedly eclectic taste, reproducing not anything large, but just such details of Peacock's work as seem to catch his fancy.

III

AN ASPECT OF THE COMIC SPIRIT

Although Meredith did not deliver his famous lecture on Comedy, which was published afterward under the title *An Essay on Comedy and the Uses of the Comic Spirit*, until 1877, the philosophy which he there so carefully expounds had long since permeated his work. Indeed, we can trace it from the very beginnings; Shagpat, his first book, shows it in clear but embryonic form. Indeed, Shagpat is especially significant because of the particular formative stage of the idea that it exhibits. Meredith there is, as yet, interested in only a single phase of the subject; namely, the therapeutic power of laughter. But, in two episodes of the book, that part of the teaching is clearly set forth. First then is the story of Noorna of Oolb, who, from her books of magic, has learned the secret wisdom, that men transformed out of their proper shape and mind can be restored to human likeness and sanity, if only they can be made to laugh. And so it is that all the birds of the enchantress Goorelka's aviary are freed from their spell and become again men after Noorna has made them laugh for the space of an hour.[1] Again this same doctrine of the corrective value of laughter is illustrated in the narrative of Shibli Bagarag's escape from the hall of Aklis where, as a result of his folly, he sat immovable upon a throne, crowned with a crown of jewelled monkey-skulls and asses'-ears.[2] But here the teaching has a new application, for this time laughter is shown as the efficient instrument of self-criticism. It was because Shibli, beholding his absurd self in a mirror, could laugh heartily at his own plight, that he was able to escape from bondage. Immediately, when he laughed, he was freed from his compulsory seat, able once more to go upon his questing.

Nor does this presentation of the Comic idea disappear after *Shagpat*. Meredith returns to it again in *Richard Feverel* where he

---

[1] *The Shaving of Shagpat*, Vol. I, pp. 162–176.
[2] *The Shaving of Shagpat*, Vol. I, p. 207.

tells quite explicitly that it was just the lack of this self-directed laughter that made Sir Austen his own lasting victim. "He could catch at times," writes Meredith, "very humorous glances at the broad reflection which the world of fact . . . holds up for us." (The figure here recalls immediately Shibli's mirror.) "Unhappily the faculty of laughter which is due to this gift, was denied him. For a good wind of laughter had relieved him of much of the blight of self-deception, and oddness, and extravagance; had given him a healthier view of the atmosphere of life; but he had it not."[3] Such is the limited, but lucid, and psychologically sound, teaching of the Comic Idea in its earlier appearance.

It is to be noted that Meredith's idea of laughter, at this stage, is remarkably like that of Peacock who in many places praises laughter as an aid in the wise conduct of life. "The world is a stage, and life is a farce, and he that laughs most, has most profit of the performance," he makes Friar Turk affirm in a passage of *Maid Marian* often quoted as setting forth Peacock's fundamental philosophy.[4] Again, in *Nightmare Abbey*, in like spirit, he makes Mr. Hilary, who, as his name indicates, is a cheery person, declare "the highest wisdom and the highest genius have been invariably accompanied by cheerfulness."[5] And so it is throughout all Peacock; everywhere the laughing man is shown to be the superior. The resemblance here to Meredith's conception of laughter as a renovating agent in a psychological process is clear. Meredith and Peacock both identify laughter with the power of self-examination, which is the center of sanity, and with joy, which is the outward token or sign of sanity. And Meredith, at first, like Peacock, scarcely goes beyond this. His attention still is upon laughter in relation to the individual alone; the social implications of laughter in a wider sense, the cosmic aspect of the Muse, is as yet untouched upon. He has not yet set up that Spirit of Comedy, which, personified, stands far above mankind as a whole, watching men both collectively and individually, and mocking with distant laughter their antic foibles. That conception was for the future to bring forth.

---

[3] *The Ordeal of Richard Feverel*, Vol. 2, Ch. XXII, pp. 194–95
[4] *Maid Marion*, Ch. XVI, p. 125.
[5] *Nightman Abbey*, Ch. XI, p. 213.

The figure of the Comic Spirit as it is later developed is interesting because of the tentative shapes in which at first it was cast. The figure of the Muse even to the end remains somewhat elusive; yet we come to know *her*, through casual indications, eventually, as a serene, young Goddess, one of Meredith's clear-eyed young women, perhaps, raised to divinity, a Muse like those of the classic Nine. Such, however, is the final appearance of the Comic Spirit. In the earlier novels her place and function is assumed by lesser creatures; by mocking gods, and howling imps. These, in fact, are her proto-types. It is in *Richard Feverel* that we hear of the laughing gods; and quite appropriately it is Adrian Harley, "the wise youth," that hears them. It is of him that we are told:—[6] "the fine aristocrats of literature (Horace and Gibbon) helped him to accept humanity as it had been, and was, a supreme ironic procession with the laughter of gods in the back-ground. Why not the laughter of mortals also?"

Such a conception, as we hope to show, is strangely Peacockian, repeating a *motif* that Peacock had used in fantasy several times. But Meredith evidently was not satisfied with it. Seemingly Meredith was experimenting with personifications for his Comic Spirit, for although the idea of the laughing Goddess is projected in *Evan Harrington*, it is for the time abandoned; and in *The Egoist* "little scoundrel imps—dogs and pets of the Comic Spirit—set forth to watch mankind," are introduced.[7] It is these imps, so like a medieval troop of besetting personal devils, that gather around the unhappy Willoughby Patterne, all unconscious of their presence, and "whose fits of roaring first made mild angels (Clara and Laetitia) aware of something comic in him." In the sly, uncouth behavior of these creatures there is more than a trace of an earlier Peacockian conception. Meredith, however, must have found the imps as unsatisfactory for his purpose as had proved the earlier gods; for he abandons them and permanently reinstates the figure of the divinely witted-woman in their stead. The transformation is striking; indeed, there is something incongruous about it; as though a

---

[6] *The Ordeal of Richard Feverel*, Vol. 2, Ch. I, p. 8.
[7] *The Egoist*, Vol. 13, Ch. II, p. 10.

Caliban had suddenly been transmogrified into an Ariel. But such is the evolution.

As has been said before, Meredith's earlier conception of the laughter of the gods is interesting because it provides a link to the work of Peacock, and hints that Meredith's perfected and elaborate philosophy of the Comic may have had a point of origination in the ideas of his father-in-law. This notion is enforced by the observation that Peacock, in his work both early and late, introduces something very akin to the Comic Spirit. Both in its manifestation and idea this spirit is so like Meredith's as to sugfest a relationship, not only possible but extremely probable.

In *Gryll Grange* (1861), his last novel, Peacock introduced a farce entitled *Aristophanes in London*,[8] which, as an amateur theatrical, is produced by the whole company spending Christmas at the Grange for part of their holiday entertainment. The plot of the piece, which is intended to satirize "progress" and "the march of mind," always matters with Peacock for ridicule, is quite simple. A group of "controls" in the Spirit-rapping Society in London call back from the dead the shades of Circe and Gryllus, who have reposed three thousand years; also a number of later worthies, including Hannibal, Coeur de Lion, and Cromwell, with the purpose of persuading them to acknowledge the greater glory of the present age. To these assembled spirits are exhibited all the wonders of the day: trains, steamships, and gas illumination. The ghosts, however, remain strangely unimpressed; they refuse to admit any superiority in modern man and his works. Finally, the discomfiture of the complacent spirit rappers is made complete by a huge, derisive guffaw that rings about them.

> "What," asks a spirit-rapper, "is that wondrous
> Sound that seems like thunder,
> Mixed with gigantic laughter?"
> To which question Circe replies:
> "It is Jupiter,
> Who laughs at your presumption, half in anger,
> And half in mockery."

Gryll Grange, Ch. XXVIII, pp. 213–226.

Here surely is a perfect parallel to that laughter of the gods accompanying "the supreme, ironic procession of humanity," of which we hear in *Richard Feverel*.[9] Both evidently look back to common sources, probably the same great original, Aristophanes *Clouds*, which Peacock, himself, so manifestly used for the basis of his Christmas farce at the Grange. Meredith we know, from his appreciative references to Aristophanes in the *Essay on Comedy*, was like Peacock an admirer of the Greek dramatist and a student of his work.[10] Accordingly it is interesting to speculate how much of Meredith's interest in Aristophanes had been stimulated by the enthusiasm of Peacock. The publication of *Richard Feverel* (1859), prior to *Gryll Grange* (1861) makes it clear the influence, if it existed, must have come from an earlier time; for, at that date, no personal relationship any longer existed between Meredith and Peacock, that having passed with the defection of Mary Meredith. As it happens there is evidence to show from Peacock's earlier period that the possibility of such an influence had existed; that in fact Meredith had the opportunity of reading Aristophanic farce of Peacock's own writing.

The possible influence of Peacock's two fragmentary novels, *Caleidore*, and another without title which, however, Mr. Richard Garnett, owner of the manuscript, calls *Lord of the Hills* has hitherto been overlooked.[10] They would seem, however, to be particularly significant as connecting links between the comedies of Aristophanes and Peacock, on the one hand; and Peacock and Meredith, on the other. They hint, at once, both at an immediate and an ultimate source for Meredith's philosophy of the Comic Muse, tying Meredith to Peacock, and through Peacock to the classical sources that were Peacock's own. In this respect they are highly significant.

The story of *Caleidore*, which Mr. Garnett dates about 1816,[11] embodies the same idea as *Aristophanes in London;* namely the coming to London of a prince from the dwelling of the ancient

---

[9] *An Essay on Comedy and the Uses of the Comic Spirit*, Vol. 23, pp. 35–38.
[10] See Peacock's fragmentary novels in *Thomas Love Peacock: Letters to Edward Hookham and Percy Bysthe Shelley with Fragments of Unpublished Manuscripts*, edited by Richard Garnett, Boston, 1910, pp. 141–250.
[11] *Ibid.*, see preface by Mr. Garnett.

gods of Greece, the Terra Incognita, where too, we are told, King Arthur and his knights have taken refuge. This stranger who invokes the pagan deities and asks the Vicar of Llangasrhyd for his daughter in the names of Juno, Venus and Cupid, in spite of his good manners, is a shocking anomaly, an *enfant terrible*, let loose in our modern society to expose its defects. Unhappily Peacock, surprised by the difficulties he had set himself, did not complete *Calidore*. Still, fragmentary as it is, the intention of the piece is plain: to show forth the follies of our life as they must appear to one of god-like intelligence coming, innocent, among us.

Interesting as *Calidore* is, the other fragment, *Lord of the Hills*, is even more striking because in it the idea of the Comic Spirit is stated explicitly, in such clear terms as to be unmistakable. It is, indeed, the Meredithian concept anticipated quite fully. Strangely enough the background, the characters, and the atmosphere of the scene, as distinguished from mere scenery, all suggest another author, most unclassical in spirit, and one having nothing to do with the Comic Spirit or its ways; namely, Mrs. Anne Radcliffe, author of *The Mysteries of Udolpho* and *The Italian*. It must be remarked, however, that this is not surprising, since traces of Mrs. Radcliffe's influence are to be met with occasionally in other of Peacock's novels, especially in the handling of description. *Nightmare Abbey* has definite affiliations with the castle in *The Mysteries of Udolpho;* and in *Melincourt* and elsewhere, in descriptions of rugged mountain scenery, the landscape of Mrs. Radcliffe is often suggested. It is most likely, because Peacock chose to think of his laughing spirit as a rather formidable creature, of lurking ways and of covert purpose, of a nature more than human, that he saw fit to introduce him amid a Radcliffian setting, at once glamorous and forbidding, hinting of mystery and peril.

The story of *The Lord of the Hills* is briefly told. A party of French people, M. and Mme. de Virelai, with their daughter Adeline and servant Elsie, are benighted in a romantic mountain pass between Bohemia and Silesia. Mme. de Virelai, although from skeptical Paris, believes in the existence of Numbernip, a wandering spirit who dwells in those parts. She wants to see or, at least, to hear him; so does her daughter, Adeline. M. de Virelai, however, is skeptical of the creature's existence; as is, likewise, their hostess of the inn. Presently, while they are still discussing the existence of Numbernip, an elderly officer and a sportsman enter the house. The two parties join, and after a pleasant dinner, the elderly officer, who has overheard the discussion concerning Numbernip, tells them his experiences with the demon.

As a young man, on his journey to Paris to join the forces of the Revolution, he had passed through those same mountains. Fatigued, he had sat down to rest awhile upon a certain stone. And as he sat, his mind all aglow with dreams of liberty and of social progress, he had eagerly anticipated all the high actions in which he was soon to bear a part. It was then that he heard behind him, for the first time, the echoing laughter of a mocking voice. In later years, passing that way again, he had sat once more upon that stone. But now he was an officer of the Grand Army of France, and he dreamed of the conquest of empire upon which shortly Napoleon would lead his soldiery. Again, for the second time, the mocking voice nearby had rung in his ears. So it had been: whenever in that spot he had sat to meditate on any delusion of life, any mirage of glory, always that voice had mocked his dream. But, now, said the officer, he was old, without delusions; and the voice laughed for him no more. M. de Virelai, interested by the account, himself, the following morning, sitting down in the proper place, voiced his modest hope of human progress. Whereupon the voice roared in his ears, most disconcertingly.

Is not this spirit Numbernip much like the Meredithian Comic Spirit? His name has meaning: Numbernip, he who "nips" or mocks at many. The individual and, beyond the individual and through him, all humanity are his victims. But not only in the spirit and direction of his malice is this wood-god of Peacock's like Meredith's; this elusive spirit in its physical aspect and habits too, foreshadows Meredith's later creation. Indeed, it may be said that Meredith has pictured identically the same creature in the fine brief description of the Comic Spirit which he gives toward the close of his famous lecture. To compare Meredith's nameless Spirit as it is imaged there with Peacock's Numbernip is to discover an analogy which is amazing in its completeness, point for point. But let the passage tell its own story.[12]

> If you believe, writes Meredith, that our civilization is founded in commonsense (and it is the first condition of sanity to believe it), you will, when contemplating men, discover a Spirit overhead; not more heavenly than the light flashed upward from glassy surfaces, but luminous and watchful; never shooting beyond them or lagging in the rear; so closely attached to them that it may be taken for a slavish reflex, until its features are studied. It has the sages' brows, and the sunny malice of a faun lurks at the corners of the half-closed lips drawn in an idle wariness of half tension. The slim feasting smile, shaped like the long-bow, was once a big round satyr's laugh that flung up the brows like a fortress lifted by gunpowder. The laugh will come again, but it will be of the order of the smile, finely tempered, showing sunlight of the mind, mental richness rather than noisy enormity. Its common aspect is one of unsolicitous observation, as if surveying a full field and having leisure to dart on its chosen morsels, without any fluttering eagerness. Men's future upon earth does not attract it; their honesty and shapeliness in the present does; and whenever they wax out of proportion, over-blown, affected, pretentious, bombastical, hypocritical, pedantic, fantastically delicate; whenever it sees them self-deceived or hood-winked, given to riot in idolatries, drifting into vanities, congregating in absurdities, planning short sightedly, plotting dementedly; whenever they are at variance with their professions, and violate the unwritten but perceptible laws binding them in consideration one to another; whenever they offend sound reason, sane justice, are false in humility or mined with conceit, individually, or in the bulk— the Spirit overhead will look humanely malign, and cast an oblique light on them, followed by volleys of silvery laughter. That is the Comic Spirit.

Out of the passage, from beneath the heaped-up words of emphatic repetition, the image that emerges is clear; it is of a creature the very self of Numbernip, Peacock's invention of fifty years earlier. The resemblance can scarcely be accidental:

---

[12] *An Essay on Comedy and the Uses of the Comic Spirit*, Vol. 23, pp. 46–47.

both the image and the idea that it embodies are alike; and chance likeness could hardly extend so far. Evidently it is the resuscitation of a memory from Meredith's earlier impressionable days when he had access to Peacock's unpublished MSS. That Meredith should revert for a striking personification of the Comic Spirit, so long after, to Peacock's figure is not surprising, for Numbernip is not easily forgotten. The point is, however, that, no matter what its other sources, the philosophy of the Comic Spirit as developed by Meredith does have an origination in Peacock. Although the product of evolution, as evidenced by the changing forms in which Meredith pictures it, it throws back in its general philosophy definitely to Peacock; there at least it finds one sturdy and easily traceable root.

IV

OF SENTIMENTALISM AND ITS CURE

Closely allied to the workings of the Comic Spirit is the subject of Sentimentalism, one of the most common of those forms of false feeling and thinking that it is the function of laughter to rebuke. This, again, is a subject upon which both Peacock and Meredith are entirely agreed, and to which both have given considerable attention in their work. Peacock's most definite pronouncement upon the theme is found in his provocative, paradoxical essay *The Four Ages of Poetry* (1820) which he wrote to bait Shelley, and which succeeded so well in its purpose that the far more famous *Defence of Poetry* was written as an answer to it. It is toward the close of his essay that Peacock gives a definition of sentimentalism which, as has been pointed out,[1] defines perfectly the theme of *The Egoist*, and, indeed, sentimentalism, as an idea, wherever it appears in Meredith. But beyond the exactness of the definition of "sentiment", as Peacock calls it, the passage is interesting in a wider sense. Peacock, who was himself a poet, was, of course, writing tongue in cheek when he declared that there was no place for poetry in a progressing world. But he was sincerely indignant at, what was popularly passing as poetry in his own day. It was the debased taste of the public, and the pandering to it by the poetasters that were the real objects of his attack. He speaks of that "much larger portion of the reading public, whose minds are not awakened to the desire of valuable knowledge, and who are indifferent to anything beyond being charmed, moved, excited, affected, and exalted: charmed by harmony, moved by sentiment, excited by passion, affected by pathos, and exalted by sublimity: harmony, which is language on the rack of Procrustes; *sentiment, which is canting egoism in the mask of refined feeling;* passion, which is the commotion of a weak and selfish mind; pathos, which is the whining of an unmanly spirit; and sublimity which is the inflation of an

---

[1] Moffatt, James, *George Meredith, A Primer to the Novels*, London, 1909 p. 269.

empty head."² In such savage fashion does Peacock run down the several prevailing forms of bad taste, all of which, he shows, proceed from a tinsel and flummery appetite in the public at large—an idol powerful to pervert, which should not be catered to.

It is this same note of indignation at a public given over to fine feelings and mere prettiness that runs through Meredith's letters years later. His own literary creed was built on the same stern opposition to the tastes "of the narrow minds of the drawing room," as Peacock's. The mantle of the older man seems quite naturally to have fallen on Meredith's shoulders. Of Tennyson, whose fine natural gifts he often praised, Meredith writes in the same spirit that Peacock showed in his *Four Ages of Poetry:* "the Sir Pandarus public . . . has corrupted this fine singer. In his degraded state I really believe he is useful, for he reflects as much as our Society chooses to show of itself. The English notion of passion, virtue and valor is in his pages. Isn't there a scent of damned hypocrisy in all this lisping and vowelled purity of *The Idylls?* It is fashionable. It pleases the rose-pink ladies; it sells."³

Again, of Tennyson, he writes: "To think—it's in these days that the foremost poet of the country goes on fluting of creatures that have not a breath of vital humanity in them . . . the Euphuist's tongue, the Exquisite's leg, the Curate's moral sentiments, and the British matron and her daughter's purity of tone: so he talks, so he walks, so he snuffles; so he appears divine . . . Why, this stuff is not the Muse, it's Musery."⁴

In these passages, it would seem that the lurking, ubiquitous culprit is Sentimentalism. Indeed, in another letter to Capt. Frederick Maxse, Meredith names the evil explicitly. "You know my feelings about sentimentalists. I do not take them for the subjects of study, they would enrage me past any tolerance . . . The Tempter of Mankind has never such a grin as when he sees them mix the false and the true."⁵

Peacock's definition of Sentiment as "canting egotism in the

---

² Peacock, Thomas Love, *The Four Ages of Poetry*, Oxford, 1923, pp. 16–17,
³ *Letters*, Vol. 28, I, pp. 197–98.
⁴ *Ibid.*, 3.
⁵ *Letters*, Vol. 29, II, p. 335.

mask of refined feeling," is so Meredithian that it might have been written by Meredith himself. In its brief compass, it touches both horns of the subject: first, its essentially selfish nature; second, its delicacy in "the fine shades of feeling." Touching these points two memorable definitions of Meredith's come to mind; the first from the Pilgrim's Script of *The Ordeal of Richard Feverel:*—

"Sentimentalists are they who seek to enjoy without incurring the Immense Debtorship for a thing done";[6] the second from *Diana of the Crossways*, "They (Sentimentalists) fiddle harmonies on the strings of sensualism."[7] So far as can be judged from aphoristic utterance, the two novelists are in perfect agreement concerning the trait.

The selfishness and irresponsibility of the Sentimentalist has been delineated in the unforgettable Whilloughby Patterne of *The Egoist*, in the less convincing Lord Fleetwood of *The Amazing Marriage*, and the altogether unlovely Wilfred Pole of *Sandra Belloni* and *Vittoria*. Meredith's most terrific example, however, illustrative of the more serious dangers of the Sentimental, the story of the utter tragedy that may result from a too exclusive addiction to the "fine shades of feeling," he has presented in the persons of Purcell Barrett, and his female companion-piece, Adela Pole, of *Sandra Belloni*.

Of the dangers of the Sentimental Peacock wrote in much the same vein in his fiction, although never with the same seriousness, nor with the deepening tragic note of Meredith. In *Nightmare Abbey*, the character of Scythrop shows the pathology of the Sentimental. He is represented as the victim of a false idealism, a prey to the fashionable Byronism of the day. His melancholia has been fostered by the reading of Goethe's *Sorrows of Werther* and other German romances of that ilk. Under such unhealthful influences, he has "forgotten that there are such things as sunshine and music in the world." He has become separated from the realities of life; his normal social impulses are perverted so that he wishes only for solitude, "to wander among the venerable remains of the greatness that has passed forever."

---

[6] *The Ordeal of Richard Feverel*, Vol. 2, Ch. XXIV, p. 220.
[7] *Diana of the Crossways*, Vol. 16, Ch. I, p. 12.

All the sickly manifestations of his life are self-induced, the results of his adoption of the morbid, but fashionable philosophy of the time. In the character of Scythrop, of course, Peacock has put more than a touch of burlesque; but his difficulty, much like that of the Egoist, is born of his pampered sensibilities and false idealizations. One particular point that draws Scythrop into company with Meredith's sentimental heroes is his attempt, vainly, to hold the love of two young women at the same moment. This, it is to be remembered, is also the dilemma of Whilloughby Patterne of *The Egoist* and of Wilfred Pole of *Sandra Belloni*. Whether Meredith in exploiting this situation is following out the hint that *Nightmare Abbey* afforded, is hard to say. Peacock's treatment of Scythrop's indecision is playful, while Meredith's, although subject to the shafts of the Comic Spirit, is fundamentally serious. This difference, however, only points the opposition of temperamental bias that distinguishes the two men, always, in relation to their material. At any rate, the analogy is interesting and must be considered. The situation involved, a man's hesitancy in the bestowal of his affections, is fullest of dramatic possibilities, since it, better than all others, plumbs the heart of the sentimental victim and shows his helplessness to deal effectively with life. This obvious truth Meredith has seized on and given the most detailed treatment. Perhaps it is wholly his find; still the introduction of the lover's dilemma in Peacock, in connection with the theme of the Sentimental, suggests a likely origin for it there.

Peacock rejoins the theme of the Sentimental in studious fashion in his last novel, *Gryll Grange*. In the person of Robert Falconer he has given an analysis of the Sentimental quite as penetrating, if not so artful, as Meredith's; in some respects even more so, since he delves deep in the problem of causation. With causes of Sentimentalism, Meredith does not much concern himself; Willoughby Patterne and Lord Fleetwood are interpreted to us solely in terms of their pride, an inadequate explanation, inasmuch as a healthy passion would have pushed them out of their dilemma; and on this fundamental lack in them Meredith lays little stress. More nearly does Meredith approach a full study of the Sentimental type in the characters of Wilfred Pole and Purcell Barrett. These men, exquisites in affection, fastidious, and timorous in their respect for women, one of whom becomes a mere butterfly figure, the other, a suicide, are very like Peacock's Falconer. They are Meredith's most complete, although not his most interesting or pleasant, psychological studies.

In the character of Robert Falconer Peacock has presented us with a confirmed sentimentalist who, only by long continued pressure, is finally weaned from his folly. He is discovered by the kindly Dr. Opimian living in a very peculiar manner. His bedroom is hung around with pictures from the life of St. Catherine. The presence of these pictures and his liking for them, Falconer explains as follows:—

"The pictures of St. Catherine and her legend very early impressed her in my mind as the type of ideal beauty—of all that can charm, irradiate, refine, exalt, in the best of the better sex."[8]

To this explanation, Dr. Opimian replies very sensibly:—

"I am afraid I am too matter of fact to sympathize very clearly with this form of aestheticism . . . Your faith is simply poetical. But take care, my young friend, that you do not finish by becoming the dupe of your own mystification. . . . I hope you will not be led into investing the ideality with too much semblance of reality."

But, beyond this, Falconer is attended by seven young maids, all sisters, who in the evening gather to play and sing religious music, which always they conclude with a Latin hymn to St. Catherine.[9] It is most interesting that Meredith, in *The Amazing Marriage*, makes reference to exactly this sort of devotion; and his description, in that novel, of Lord Feltre's, Fleetwood's Catholic friend's, "religiosity", is an unmistakable recollection of Peacock's description of Falconer.[10] "Your convinced and fervent Catholic," he writes, "has quotations, and images and Latin hymns to the Madonna or one of his Catherines, by the dozen, to suit the enthusiastic fit of the worship of some fair woman." It is a tribute to the penetrating insight of both Peacock and

---

[8] *Gryll Grange*, Ch. IX, pp. 55–61.
[9] *Gryll Grange*, Ch. IV, pp. 35–37.
[10] *The Amazing Marriage*, Vol. 19, Ch. XXXVIII, p. 395.

Meredith that they should have understood the sublimating action of such worship, and gauged so accurately its place in human psychology. In this they anticipate by intuition the teachings of Freud and his school. However, our business is with the particular reference where Meredith's mention of Latin hymns and St. Catherine shows perfectly well that he had *Gryll Grange* in mind when he wrote. The parallel is too close to be merely accidental.

Falconer, as Peacock presents him, is the type of man who has entered into an almost illusory existence. Later, when he is introduced to society and the person of Morgana Gryll, a potent charmer, with whom he is half in love, he resents, very naturally, the break-up of his old life. "It must be a dreadful calamity to be in love," he exclaims,[11] feeling it imminent. "But my scheme of life was perfect," he complains to Dr. Opimian; and then goes on to explain that "he had always placed the *summum bonum* of life in tranquility, and not in excitement." In short, to quote from the much earlier *Nightmare Abbey*, he is in the plight of "a Rosicrucian who will love nothing but a sylph, who does not believe in the existence of a sylph, and who yet quarrels with the whole universe for not containing a sylph;"[12] only with the difference that even when the sylph is found, he still is uncertain about her.

In the character of Falconer the whole mechanism of the Sentimental, together with its aftermath of pernicious effects, is laid open to view. The study, as with everything in Peacock, is more descriptive and exact, than real. Peacock is not portraying in Falconer a man, but demonstrating a point of view; he is not an artist, but a clinical lecturer giving information. To that end he gives us a very interesting diagram for study. Meredith, on the other hand, is ever intent on giving a living investiture to his idea. Accordingly, we have the Egoist; or when he draws nearer to Peacock, a morbid study like that of Purcell Barrett of *Sandra Belloni*. But in both authors it is to be insisted the idea is the same. When in *The Ordeal of Richard Feverel* Mere-

---

[11] *Gryll Grange*, Ch. XII, pp. 793–802.
[12] *Nightmare Abbey*, Ch. XI, p. 212.

dith says of Sentimentalism:[13] "It is a happy pastime and an important science to the timid, the idle, and the heartless; but a damning one to them who have anything to forfeit," he is simply preaching again the straight doctrine enunciated by Peacock before him. Conversely, one is reminded after reading of Meredith's people, of the young lady of whom Peacock writes in *Melincourt*[14] "who had cultivated a great deal of *theoretical* romance—in taste, not in feeling—an important distinction." This vital distinction, the difference between the Sentimental and the Real, is a recurring theme in Peacock; Meredith's work is in expanding it, making a more insistent use of it, and embodying it as an underlying element in convincing characterization.

If the teaching of the Sentimental is clearly traced through the work of Peacock; so, almost of necessity, is its converse and complement, which becomes the positive note of Meredith's teaching: the insistence upon conformity to the teaching of Nature or Earth. The word "nature" Peacock employs in a sense entirely consonant with its repeated use by Meredith. With Peacock too it is a philosophical term, denoting no mere physical force, but that process of reality, at once physical and psychical, with which the individual must be one. When we are told of Anthelia, the heroine of *Melincourt*, that "she had always looked with calmness on the course of necessity: she felt she was always in the course of nature,"[15] we feel that here is not only the Meredithean woman, full-grown, but that here Meredith's philosophy also is anticipated. Peacock does not hesitate at times to put the words of this wisdom into the mouths of his queerest freaks; as when he makes Mr. Asterias, who searches the seven seas for a Mermaid, say of the happy man: "Nature is his great and inexhaustible treasure."[16] It is left, however, for Mr. Hilary, also of *Nightmare Abbey*, to set forth succinctly our common purpose:[17] "To reconcile man as he is to the world as it is, to

---

[13] *The Ordeal of Richard Feverel*, Vol. 5, Chap. XXIV, p. 220.
[14] *Melincourt*, Ch. II, p. 14.
[15] *Melincourt*, Ch. X, p. 79.
[16] *Nightmare Abbey*, Ch. VII, p. 186.
[17] *Nightmare Abbey*, Ch. XI, p. 213.

preserve and improve all that is good, to destroy all that is evil in moral and physical nature." It is from quotations of this sort, scattered but consistent with each other and always clear in their import, that Peacock's teaching of Nature builds itself. It is characteristic of Peacock's highest wisdom that it is usually presented incidentally to other matters and in aphoristic form; he flashes his thought before us, then passes quickly to other things. He is basically a man of theory; but Peacock, as a worldly pragmatist, does not insist on his theory. Having settled the business of living in a fashion comfortable to himself, he remarks on it but casually; proclaiming the rule of Nature only against those who too obviously flout it. Only on lesser matters, questions of the franchise, paper-money, the enclosing of common lands, can he be provoked to long, and it must be added tedious, discussion. With Meredith it is just the opposite. He is vitally interested in the central questions of philosophy, and genuinely concerned about them; accordingly, he proclaims his gospel to all who will hear. He becomes the intrusive philosopher, sometimes hiding behind a *Pilgrim's Script*, a *Book of Egoism, Journal*, or some other such device; or, again, speaking in his own person, apologizing for it sometimes, but talking on with serious didactic purpose. Peacock, on the other hand, holds his peace. His books are a kind of enlarged scrap-books in which all sorts of things are set down. He insists on nothing; wisdom, buffonery, and tedious discussion are all thrown together in a grand *mélange*. Let the reader make what he can of it, and take what he pleases. It is this difference in form and the attitude beneath it that helps to conceal many of the *rappochements* between Meredith and Peacock. Basically their ideas, considered apart from the plan and manner of their appearance, are surprisingly the same. Especially is this true in regard to the affirmative elements of Peacock's thought.

Just as Peacock and Meredith are agreed on the necessity of conformity to Nature, so too they are one in regard to the means by which that good is to be attained. Both of them insist on one thing; namely the use of intelligence as the instrument and prime aid in man's redemption from error. "The only source of freedom is intellectual light," Peacock makes his dreary economist, Mr. Fax, declare.[18] "The ignorant are always slaves though they dwell among the Andes. The wise are all free though they cultivate a savannah." Again, he pronounces, "The qualities of heart and mind are alone out of the power of accident." Speaking in his own person in his preface to the second edition of *Melincourt* (1856) Peacock writes: "Strenuous idleness drives us on the wings of steam, seeking the art of enjoying life which, after all, is in the regulation of the mind, and not in the whisking about of the body."[19] Although it must be admitted that in putting such stress on the primacy of mind Peacock, in part, was moved by a purely scholarly interest, the dilettante's fear that in a mechanized age humane studies might become altogether obsolete; still his advocacy was prompted, at bottom, by the deeper consideration, his philosophical belief, that only by intelligence can man be emancipated from cramping social tyrannies and all the vain illusions that spring up from them. With him, as with Meredith, it was basic doctrine[20] "that the world of reality is not the world of romance," that man can flourish only in Reality, and that "a healthy mind in a healthy body" is the only condition of human well-being.[21] The difference between the two is purely in the degree of their insistence upon the teaching.

The ideal of the man of thought is much further developed in Meredith, who is much more severely intellectual than his father-in-law. In the simple intuitions of the heart Peacock placed great confidence; indeed, in spite of his skepticism, an almost childlike faith. But of these Meredith is less trustful. The mere motion of the blood is not of itself to be believed. Accordingly, Meredith, although he has celebrated the companioning of "blood and brain and spirit, three," and in such passages as the well-known exposition of love in *Diana* insists on the equal value of physical and psychical elements with the intellectual as the criteria of human guidance, for the actual conduct of life seems to have trusted mind to an almost unbelievable degree. One cannot but agree with Marcel Schwobe that the message of

---

[19] *Melincourt*, reprint of Peacock's preface to the edition of 1856, p. 2.
[20] *Melincourt*, Ch. XII, p. 91.
[21] *Gryll Grange*, Ch. XXI, p. 158.

Meredith may well be summed up in the one sentence:[22]—
"'More brain, O Lord, more brain;' more brain for woman
to understand man; more brain for man to understand Nature."
The surprising measure of Meredith's reliance upon, and faith in,
intellect can, perhaps, be apprehended best from his letters.
To his son, Arthur, for example, he writes,[23] "My aim, and I
trust it will be yours, is never to take counsel of my sensations;
but of my intelligence." Indeed, on occasion, he seems almost
to over-reach himself; one can scarcely help thinking of Lady
Blandish's comment on Sir Austen in *Richard Feverel*:[24] "He
tries to be more than he is." The exaggeration, however, is but
for the moment, and is explained by remembrance of the conditions which are the cause of the heavy counter-stroke: that
"Society . . . kept in animation by the customary . . . and
by Sentiment;"[25] that Society which further he describes as
giving "ear to those who shiver at things as they are; not seeing
that a frank acceptance of Reality is the firm basis of the ideal."

Quite rightly has Meredith been called the apostle of idealistic
naturalism; his teaching is of Nature, not Nature half seen and
unbridled, but Nature known and dominated by a wakeful
intelligence. This is the great positive note of practical philosophy that sounds crescendo through all his work. Accordingly,
its anticipation in Peacock, with all the main threads of its
development intact, is provocative of speculation. To analyse
and resolve all the formative elements of Meredith's final philosophy is, of course, impossible. Their number and variety, it goes
without saying, is great. There are of course, other bonds
over-seas, with Goethe in Germany;[26] other bonds close at home,
in sundry quarters. Nevertheless, in view of the parallelism of
their ideas, it would seem more than a guess, more than a possible inference that there was between him and Peacock a particularly heavy traffic of ideas on the subject of man and his
adjustment to life, ideas that Meredith was to fix centrally
both in his own life and in the lives of his fictional characters.

---

[22] Hammerton, J. A., *George Meredith*, Edinburgh, 1911, p. 359.
[23] *Letters*, Vol. 28, I, p. 213.
[24] *The Ordeal of Richard Feverel*, Vol. 2, Ch. XXXVII, p. 417.
[25] *Letters*, Vol. 29, II, p. 607.
[26] Lee, John, *George Meredith's Literary Relations with Germany*, MLR., October, 1917.

V

THE SPECTACLE OF ENGLAND

Significant among other points of similarity between Meredith and Peacock is the essential agreement of their social view. The England of Peacock's day was, of course, not the England of Meredith's day, and many of the contemporary issues which interested the elder man are exchanged in Meredith for others, equally transient. Moreover, it must be admitted that the courses of their political affiliations do not coincide. Peacock himself, in respect to politics, early and late, is something of a parodoxical figure, a man standing in no fixed place, at once the friend and enemy of both Radical and Tory. Seen, however, in their extended length, the political opinions of Peacock show a slow transition, faltering and never completed, from those of a Republican to those of a complacent Conservative. In Meredith, this process is, if anything, reversed. In his early years Meredith's liberal views were not so insistent that he could not, as corresponding editor, write the leaders for the Conservative *Ipswich Journal*.[1] And, although throughout his career he called himself a Liberal, it was not until the last years of his life that he entered by personal participation into the Liberal cause, going to the polls and expressing himself publicly in the press.[2] So it was that Meredith's political period came late; his political interests gained force and became militant with the years. With Peacock we have seen the opposite; less and less, apparently, did he care for those things; his crusading spirit dying away to a mere echo of its earlier satiric clamor.

However, in spite of these superficial differences, apart from particular enthusiasms, it must be repeated that in the bed-rock of their social attitude the two novelists are much alike. If Meredith becomes politically demonstrative, it does not argue that his later views of English society were sanguine with the

---

[1] Hammerton, J. A., *George Meredith*, Edinburgh, 1911, p. 14.
[2] *Ibid.*, p. 42.

hope of any immediate good; and, conversely, Peacock's later quiet ease in the view of social questions does not argue a disregard of them. In their social philosophy, despite their shifting interests, and their very different accent, Peacock and Meredith are much the same, for both are realists whose ideals are restrained by fact, and who proceed to their study of British society from identical premises.

Of the two, Peacock, perhaps because of his larger sharing in practical affairs, is the more cynical; a term scarcely to be applied to Meredith at all. Indeed, Peacock seems very much like his honest politician in *Melincourt* who told of himself: "In my ordinary intercourse with the world I reduce practice to theory; it is a habit, I believe, peculiar to myself, and a source of inexhaustible amusement."[3] Quite naturally a philosophy deduced so realistically could scarcely be other than cynical. Peacock is a man like Rochefoucault, intellectually persuaded that the selfish interest of the individual in the motive of every act and the cause behind every social institution: the State, the Church, the caste system of society. It is this belief which lies behind Mr. Fax' statement: "There is not one person in ten thousand who knows what liberty means, or cares a straw for any happiness but his own."[4] It is the belief that makes Robin Hood exclaim, "You say might overcomes right? I say no. There is no right but might."[5] Again it is the source of his cynical comment upon truth, "which, every wise man knows ought to be left to those who can get anything by it."[6]

It is interesting, however, to notice in the three passages just quoted from three different novels that, in spite of the force of the cynical declaration, such terms as "liberty", "right" and "truth" still find their place: evidently Peacock's idealism was scarcely to be snuffed out in spite of his devastating findings. Accordingly, Peacock as a realist is a somewhat bitter and protesting one. To Dr. Folliott's sentiment, "Sir, we are all brethren," he returns the answer, "Yes, sir, as the hangman is of the thief; the squire of the poacher; the judge of the libeller;

---

[3] *Melincourt*, Ch. XXI, p. 162.
[4] *Melincourt*, Ch. V, p. 39.
[5] *Maid Marion*, Ch. XI, p. 83.
[6] *Crotchet Castle*, Ch. XIV, p. 266.

the lawyer of his client; the stateman of the colleague; the bubble-blower of the bubble-buyer."[7] It is from the crossing of opinion in such passages as this, that Peacock stands out as a man, like Dickens, of large, quick sympathies, who saw and knew the injustices of society through their whole gamut, but who, unlike Dickens, sought, at least, to accept them. Peacock was, undoubtedly, the better able to do this, because, in the first place, his perceptions were intellectual rather than emotional; and, secondly, because as a member of the privileged class, comfortable and loving all sorts of luxuries, he could scarcely protest against his own fortune.

It was this perception which prevented him from being a social recusant, and which finally tempted him to resist all innovation. Peacock understood as well as any man the good that flows equally with evil from the strife of the classes. When he defines civilization as "just respect for property,"[8] there is hardly more than a dash of satire in the remark. His respect for property as the foundation stone of the amenites of life is sure. Of this aspect of universal selfishness he became the defender. "The one golden rule of right [is] to keep what we have, and to catch what we can." So says the robber, Robin Hood.[9] In *Crochet Castle* the defence is more positive. For the economic doctrines of the school of Adam Smith, Peacock had scant respect. "My principles, sir, in these things are, to take as much as I can get, and pay no more than I can help. . . . There, sir, is political economy in a nut-shell." Such is Dr. Opimian's refutation of the Scotch economist, Mr. MacQuedy.[10] Coupled with this respect for money, and concurrence in the way of the world for getting it, is a respect for those who possess it. "Good and respectable, sir, I take it, mean rich?" asks the stranger (Capt. Fitzchrome) in *Crotchet Castle*, after hearing Dr. Opimian's description of the Crotchets. "That is their meaning,' replies the good clergyman without hesitation.[11] But, we hear

---

[7] *Crotchet Castle*, Ch. VII, pp. 209–10.
[8] *Crotchet Castle*, Ch. III, p. 162.
[9] *Maid Marian*, Ch. XII, p. 88.
[10] *Crotchet Castle*, Ch. II, p. 152.
[11] *Crotchet Castle*, Ch. III, p. 162.

even more of the matter: "Decent is the distinction from respectable. Respectable means rich, and decent means poor."[12] It is in this interest that government was invented "to spend a percentage,"[13] and the laws were made "for the profit of somebody,"[14] and that morals were made "to give color to their laws."[15] Such is the system; and Peacock does not protest against it because it is owing to it, as he knows, that he himself can enjoy "a good library, a good dinner, a pleasant garden," the humane conditions of existence for himself.

This materialism, the recognition that the possession of a degree of wealth is the only soil out of which the amenities of life may grow, is as fundamental to Meredith as to Peacock. He, like Peacock, does not blink that fact. In true Peacockian vein, he writes: "Property is ballast as well as treasure. I call property funded good sense. I would give it every privilege." Both in tone and phrase the passage is reminiscent. But Meredith goes further; he explains,[16] "Now, when one really hates gold, one is at war with one's fellows. The tide sets that way. There is no compromise: to hate it is to try to stem the flood. It happens that this is one of the temptations of the sentimentalist, who should reflect, but does not, that the fine feelers by which the iniquities of gold are so keenly discerned, are a growth due to it nevertheless." Of the humanizing effect of money on its possessors Meredith speaks in several places. Wilfred Pole, we are told, had "been fattening all his life on prosperity; the very best dish in the world."[17] And, conversely, Colney Durance, of *One of Our Conquerors*, is shown as the victim of poverty. His splenetic temper is not so much his nature, as it is the result of deprivation. Victor Radnor sums up the situation in the remark, "He might have been a wealthy man by now . . . ha! it would have genialized him."[18] From such quotations it must be clear that Meredith, like his father-in-law, was an

---

[12] *Crotchet Castle*, Ch. III, p. 170.
[13] *Crotchet Castle*, Ch. VI, p. 193.
[14] *Maid Marian*, Ch. XII, p. 91.
[15] *Maid Marian*, Ch. XVII, p. 137.
[16] *Sandra Belloni*, Vol. 4, Ch. XXII, p. 214.
[17] *Sandra Belloni*, Vol. 4, Ch. XVIII, p. 179.
[18] *One of Our Conquerors*, Vol. 17, Ch. XX, p. 225.

enlightened materialist, one who realized the civilizing influence of wealth, and, accordingly, gave it first place in his social scheme. The honesty of both men, in this respect, is refreshing. Neither of them for a moment pretends to proscribe wealth or see in it the root of all evil; rather they accept it, and, unabashedly, rejoice in it as a good.

Peacock and Meredith, however, are by no means thoroughgoing materialists. Both of them, it is true, extol wealth for culture's sake; but, on the other hand, against mere wealth for its own sake, they both protest heartily. Against the usurpation of life by things, both contend; and it is this danger to the life of England as a whole that distresses them and causes them to take alarm. In that facile optimism that predicated the Nineteenth Century as an age of Progress, a time of advance toward the Millenium, neither Peacock nor Meredith shared. Peacock, indeed, pretended to see no improvement in the time over the so-called Dark Ages. Drawing the comparison between them, he writes: "And the Nineteenth century, commonly called the enlightened age: why, I never could discover."[19] Again and again he girds at "the gigantic strides of intellect," "the march of mind," "progress", "the blessings of light," and all the other shibboleths whereby the century denominated its happy illusions.

The reason for Peacock's failure to share the enthusiasm of his age is clear enough. It was a time of invention, a mechanical age, the Industrial Revolution growing into yet more monstrous shape; and in mere machinery, no matter what its convenience, Peacock could not put his faith. Rather was his trust in the human spirit, whose cultivation he saw increasingly neglected in an age devoted to a mere material progress. Accordingly, like his Mr. Foster of *Headlong Hall*, he held forth with great energy on the subject of "roads and railways, canals and tunnels, manufacturers and machinery,"[20] but always to scoff at them. Likewise he mocked the "modern Athenians" who would teach "all the arts and sciences;" namely "steam, gas, and paper-currency."[21]

---

[19] *Melincourt*, Ch. II, p. 18.
[20] *Headlong Hall*, Ch. I, p. 9.
[21] *Crotchet Castle*, Ch. II, pp. 150–59.

For all these merely practical things, the instrumentalities of getting rather than of being, that usurped the popular interest, he had nothing but contempt, and his warfare against that sort of materialism never ceased. In fact, it seems quite probable that it was the inevitable coalition of innovating mechanics with innovating liberalism in politics that finally drove him back to the conservative camp.

The reflection of this attitude of Peacock's appears scatteredly through Meredith. It is in *Richard Feverel* that the indictment of the age first appears, couched in terms that repeat the chief charges laid against it by Peacock.[22] "An age of rampant little minds, my dear Austen," exclaims Adrian Harley, the cynic scholar. "How I hate that cant about an Age of Work—you, and your Mortons, and your parsons Brawnley, rank radicals all of you, base materialists! What does Diaper Sandoe sing of your Age of Work? Listen!

>An Age of petty tit for tat,
>   An Age of busy gabble
>An Age that's like a brewer's vat,
>   Fermenting for the rabble!
>
>An Age that drives an Iron Horse,
>   Of Time and Space defiant;
>Exulting in a Giant's Force,
>   And trembling at the Giant.
>
>An Age of Quaker hue and cut
>   By Mammon misbegotten;
>See the mad Hamlet mouth and strut
>   And mark the Kings of Cotton!
>
>From this unrest, too early wrecked,
>   A Future staggers crazy;
>Ophelia of the Ages decked
>   With woeful weed and daisy."

The verses are particularly interesting because they touch seriatim upon Peacock's chief dislikes: the Age of the Steam

---

[22] *The Ordeal of Richard Feverel*, Vol. 5, Ch. VI, pp. 48–49.

Intellect Society with the menace of the rabble rout in the background, the age of the train that uselessly[23] "whisks about men's bodies"; the age of the enslaving manufacturers. It is noteworthy that Meredith reverts to the railway and the opposition among the county aristocracy to its introduction in two of his novels: *The Egoist* and *Diana of the Crossways*. Meredith, of course, was not the enemy of the railway; it had proved its value to the general public and to him abundantly; even as it had proved it to Peacock himself long before the end of his career. But evidently here there is an echo from Peacock adopted by Meredith to illustrate the working of the conservative English mind.

In their general view of modern England, our novelists are surprisingly alike. The old cry that has echoed in the kingdom from the days of John Ball's preaching down to the present, "Things go not well in England in these days," is repeated both in Peacock and Meredith. And they both deprecate the same ills. Peacock's view is darker than Meredith's on the whole. He speaks of the proverbial phrase "Merry England" as "a phrase which must be a mirifical puzzle to anyone who looks for the first time on its present lugubrious inhabitants."[24] The morale of the people as a whole he sees at low ebb. He cannot forget that "within no great distance are divers towns, cities, and hamlets, in any of which, if you have money, you may make pretty sure of being cheated; and if you have not, quite sure of being starved—strong evidence of a state of civilization."[25] The decay of England he attributes to the mills of Yorkshire and Lancashire "with fires as eternal as those of the nether world, wherein the squalid many, from infancy to age, might be turned into component parts of machinery for the benefit of the purple-faced few." It is from such an evil time and state that he looks back to the happier, earlier ages "when they could neither poison the air with gas, nor the waters with their dregs; in short [when] they made their money of metal, and breathed pure air, and drank pure water, like unscientific barbarians."[26]

---

[23] *Melincourt*, introduction to edition of 1856, p. 2.
[24] *Misfortunes of Elphin*, Ch. XII, p. 96.
[25] *Melincourt*, Ch. IV, p. 30.
[26] *Misfortunes of Elphin*, Ch. VI, p. 40.

To the reader of Meredith such arraignment can scarcely be unfamiliar; for indeed, it lies back of all of *Beauchamp's Career*. There, even Everard Romfrey, stout Tory that he is, stands appalled at the spectacle of England. His words are memorable:[27] "You shall have a glance at the manufacturing district some day. You shall see the machines they work with. You shall see the lank-jawed, half-starved pantaloons they've managed to make of Englishmen there. My blood's past boiling; they work young children in these factories from morning to night. These manufactories are spreading like the web of the devil to suck the blood of the country. In that district an epidemic levels men like a disease in sheep. Skeletons can't make a stand," and more, useless to quote, of the same order. Again, it is Romfrey who exclaims,[28] "Manchester is the belly of the nation. . . . So long as Manchester flourishes, we're a country governed and led by the belly." It is remarkable that Meredith puts these sentiments not in the mouth of his young Radical, but, as has been noted, of a Conservative. Romfrey, standing secure in his coign of vantage, ready to fight for his privileges, yet filled with concern for the state of England, recalls Peacock. And Romfrey's position is Meredith's too; the ineffectual strivings of Beauchamp illustrate Meredith's skeptical prognosis for the success of any radical program.

It is interesting in this connection that Meredith and Peacock have each written one political novel in which the main interest centres about a Parliamentary election in a provincial town. The reference, of course, is to *Beauchamp's Career* and *Melincourt*. The election at Bevisham in many respects parallels the election at Onevote. In the first place, in each instance, the electorate is shown to be both venal and stupid. The electorate at Onevote was the more easy to secure, of course, for the simple reason that Onevote, as a rotten borough, had but one elector to be purchased. In Bevisham, a larger place, with a larger constituency, however, the same mercenary considerations are shown operating. Meredith's account of the electioneering recalls Peacock's. "In Bevisham," he writes,[29] "an election is an arrangement made

---
[27] *Beauchamp's Career*, Vol. 11, Ch. III, p. 28.
[28] *Ibid.*
[29] *Beauchamp's Career*, Vol. 11, Ch. XI, p. 105.

by Providence to square the account of the voters, and settle arrears. They reckon up the health of their two members and the chances of an appeal to the country when they fix the rents and leases. You have them pointed out to you in the streets, with the figures attached to them like titles. Mr. Tompkins, the twenty-pound man; an elector of uncommon purity." To anyone read in Peacock all this must seem quite familiar; the same satiric thrust, the very tone in the phrasing.

The fact is, quite simply, that Peacock and Meredith were both aristocrats in temper. Any sympathy that they had with the lower orders was a pity for their condition rather than a fellowly feeling for them as men. Peacock represents the citizens of Novote, the great industrial city, as the most gullible creatures in the world; and shows them as a frenzied mob chairing the M. P.'s in whose elections they have had no voice.[30] So it is with Meredith in *Beauchamp*. He represents the humble elector, if not corrupt, at least as blind to his own interests, the victim of any charlatan who may practice upon him. His feeling seems to have coincided with that of Everard Romfrey, already mentioned in this connection, who said, "Defend us from the uneducated English. The common English are doltish."[31] Accordingly, it is not surprising to find Meredith writing to Maxse,[32] "I take no interest in reform. I see no desire for it below." Or, again, "This country is Tory.[33] The party against it is a fractional party." The very indifference of the masses, and their lack of preparation for political responsibility, had fostered this skeptical attitude.

Moreover, it must be pointed out that neither Peacock nor Meredith could take the spectacle of politics very seriously. Peacock treats it definitely as an inconsequent matter, good stuff for farce. The introduction in his *Melincourt* of Sir Oran Haut-ton, a Senegambian ape, as candidate for a Parliamentary seat, shows that he regarded the whole political game as matter for laughter rather than tears. The passing off of Sir Oran as a

---

[30] *Melincourt*, Ch. XXII, pp. 168–181.
[31] *Beauchamp's Career*, Vol. 11, Ch. XLV, p. 519.
[32] *Letters*, Vol. 28, I, p. 306.
[33] *Ibid.*

British peer, is a *tour de force* of burlesque; in its implications it cuts deep: a more telling arraignment of the intellectual acumen of the British public and its rulers could scarcely be conceived, although the account remains good-natured and is singularly free from the bitterness so common in satire. It is this spirit of free laughter that Peacock passes on to Meredith. Speaking in his own person in *Beauchamp*, Meredith the philosopher comments: "At present I believe it to be their opinion (the people's), their wise opinion, and the sole opinion to a majority of them, that it is more salutary, besides more diverting, to have the fools of the kingdom represented than not."[34] It is on that note of acquiescence that both Peacock and Meredith rest their political case. There is protest in it, it is true, but there is more of a smile and a shrug of the shoulders at things that cannot easily be changed.

The analogue between Meredith and Peacock which unites their social program in its conclusions, is their common advocacy of a kind of benevolent paternalism. It is a chivalric ideal, and Meredith in *The Amazing Marriage* pretends to laugh at it: "the nobles of England leading the shoemakers of England." However, it is with him the answer to the problem of social leadership as it was with Peacock before him. When Sir Austen Feverel asserts that "the clear duty of a man of any wealth is to serve the people as best he can,"[35] he is giving expression to this idea that, fleetingly, is expressed by Meredith in many places. Everard Romfrey in *Harry Richmond*, Victor Radnor in *One of Our Conquerors*, and even Willoughby Patterne, the Egoist, h as a perception of such a duty toward his tenants, his people. "Treat the people kindly, be civil, be generous and all will be well," Meredith seems to say through these his spokesmen. It happens that this social prescription is Peacock's also. After all the argumentation and wrangling over social problems which fills so large a part of his pages, he gives in *Melincourt* what we may assume is his own answer in the picture of Mr. Forrester's generous overlordship of a contented peasantry.[36] This prospect of a

---

[34] *Beauchamp's Career*, Vol. 11, Ch. XVIII, p. 281.
[35] *The Ordeal of Richard Feverel*, Vol. 11, Ch. XXV, p. 229.
[36] *Melincourt*, Chs. XII to XIV, inclusive.

population of prosperous cottagers living under the care of a fatherly landlord is his remedy for the economic and social ills of the nation. And it he seems to have passed on to Meredith. Such a program, scarcely more than the championing of an enlightened feudalism, was hardly consonant with the spirit of Peacock's time; even less so with Meredith's. Yet Meredith retains it. Victor Radnor, he tells us, simply by talking to his striking workmen in direct manly fashion was able to get them to work; more—work with a will. Meredith explains the phenomenon briefly: "We have in large patches of these islands, a Saxon population, much wanting assistance if they are not to feel themselves beaten and driven, caught by the neck, yoked and heavy-headed. Blest, then, is he who gives them a pride of standing on legs."[37] It is this sort of paternalism that is common to both Peacock and Meredith; it is the single conclusion of their social thinking. Apart from its old-fashioned, even antique complexion, it is exactly what we should expect from two such aristocratic, yet socially-minded spirits.

One trait of the English people, among others, that drew the attention of both Peacock and Meredith, and concerning which they have written in practically identical terms, is the humanitarian impulse as it prompts the nation to an interest in reform abroad; while, obtusely, it neglects evils close at home. It is appropriate that the matter should be projected in the two political novels, *Melincourt* and *Beauchamp's Career*, that have so many points in common. In *Melincourt* Peacock, through the organization of the Anti-Saccharine Society, satirically comments upon the sentimental interest of the English in endeavoring, so long as their purses and comforts remained unaffected, to secure humane treatment for the black slaves in the sugar plantations of the Indies.[38] Meanwhile, great evils at home pass all unnoticed, except by the quixotic Mr. Forrester, who is as much knight-errant as Meredith's Beauchamp. In *Harry Richmond* also the subject recurs. Harry, telling of his childhood friend, John Thresher, typical Anglo-Saxon yeoman, says, "Even as a child I felt that he was peculiarly an

---

[37] *One of Our Conquerors*, Vol. 17, Ch. XX, P. 227.
[38] *Melincourt*, Ch. XXVII, pp. 206–11.

Englishman. Tales of injustice done on the Niger River would flush him in a heat of wrath till he cried out for fresh taxes to chastise the villains. Yet at the sight of beggars at his own gate he groaned at the taxes existing."[39]

It is interesting that both Peacock and Meredith are very much of an opinion in diagnosing this inconsistency, the flat contradiction between theory and action, which they see as one of the people's major ailments. Meredith, in one of his letters, has given a brief but telling summary of the causes as he understood them. "As far as I can observe," he writes, "the heart of the nation is Teuton and moral, and therewith intellectually obtuse, next to speechless."[40] Of this morality and its worth he has expressed himself in another place. "When the English are beaten in things material—and I do not underrate them—what is left? Their morality they will say. But contemplate it! A sourness cannot be spiritual."[41] It is of such "sour" morality that Peacock wrote in many a biting, satiric line. Unconscious hypocrisy, sanctified as a national trait, is to him, as to Meredith, a matter for a saddened mirth. "It is recorded in the Triads," he writes in *The Misfortunes of Elphin*, that "Gwrgi Garwlwyd killed a male and female of the Cymry daily, and devoured them; and, on Saturday, he killed two of each, that he might not kill on Sunday! This can only be a type of some sanctimonious hero, who made a cloak of piety for oppressing the poor."[42]

Again, probing the same fault, he writes aphoristically: "Men carry their religion in other men's heads, and their morality in their own pockets."[43] The utterance is memorable not only for its point but because of the relation it predicates between materialism and formal religion. The conflict between the instinctive moral sense of the English and greed of riches which, left merely to itself, or directed by a genuine spiritual leadership, might draw to a healthy conclusion, is shown by Peacock to be juggled into a smug compromise thanks to the offices of religious ortho-

---

[39] *The Adventures of Harry Richmond*, Vol. 9, Ch. III, p. 32.
[40] *Letters*, Vol. 28, I, 322.
[41] *Letters*, Vol. 29, II, 420.
[42] *Misfortunes of Elphin*, Ch. VI, p. 45.
[43] *Melincourt*, Ch. V, p. 40.

doxy. Peacock, in short, is the enemy of organized religion, both Anglican and Dissenting; and sees in the clergy the abettors of the hypocritical complacency to which the people are prone. And Meredith follows him perfectly in this track. Indeed, of the two, Meredith is the bitterer; for never to the end did Meredith relent against the Church. In his later works, Peacock's clerical opposition, like his political, had somewhat abated; his reverend gentlemen-scholars, Dr. Folliott and Dr. Opimian, are evidently men after his own heart; and belong to an entirely different species from Dr. Larynx, Mr. Grovelgrub, and Mr. Portpipe, the ignorant, servile parsons of his earlier period. However, in the main, Peacock may be written down as definitely, even violently, anti-clerical. His later sympathetic representations of the clergy would seem to betoken an admiration for a type of man, rather than for an institution; although it is possible that toward the Church itself he experienced change of feeling.

Meredith's opposition to the Church goes back, as he tells us, to memories of his youth, of insufferable sermons sat through under prosy preachers.[44] And the liberal influence of the school at Neuwied, of course, had large place in his emancipation from religious ties that chafed.[45] Accordingly, in Peacock, scoffer of the clergy, he was prepared, when he met him, to find a congenial spirit. At any rate, there can be little doubt that Meredith was influenced by Peacock's example in drawing his own pictures of the clergy. It is noteworthy that he follows Peacock in creating two types of clergymen. He can draw, as we have seen elsewhere, the likeness of the scholar-clergyman as well as Peacock himself; but more often, he prefers to show the less estimable type; and here the influence of Peacock is particularly noticeable. His clergy are never distinguished like Peacock's for their grossness, their voracious appetite and sodden animalism. Their other characteristics, however, the mind impenetrably closed, and pliancy to wealth, are presented. Moreover, his general attitude toward the profession is strikingly like Pea-

---

[44] *Letters*, Vol. 28, I, p. 40.
[45] Selincourt, R. E., *The Life of George Meredith*, New York, 1929, p. 9.

cock's. Peacock has represented, except in *Crotchet Castle* and *Gryll Grange*, the clergy as wasters, a burden upon the land, sycophantic to the great and indifferent to the poor. It is with this thought that Meredith writes of them in *Beauchamp's Career*, making his hero say, "these thirty or forty thousand [the Clergy], Colonel, call the men that do the work they ought to be doing demagogues. The parsonry are to be absolutely counted on for waste as to progress."[46] Indeed, the chief difference in Meredith's treatment of the clergy as distinguished from Peacock's, is in his ill-suppressed irritation when dealing with the subject. Where Peacock lavished ridicule, making his parsons mere buffoons, Meredith, although less brutal, becomes caustic; beneath his finesse there shows a flush of anger. But in the reasoning of their opposition they are much alike.

Apart from the political criticism which Meredith, following Peacock, threw into his political novels, he has used for that same purpose forms employed by Peacock. In his dialogues, *Up to Midnight*,[47] written for the *Graphic* (1872-3), he imitated in straightforward fashion the political dialogue as it appears characteristically in Peacock; and in the so-called "phantasies."[48], *The Rajah in London* and *The Delphica Episode*, both of which appear in *One of Our Conquerors*, he imitates the Peacockian interlude, of which the great example is *Aristophanes in London* in *Gryll Grange* (1861).[49]

The dialogues constituting *Up to Midnight* are interesting not only because in them Meredith is patiently imitating Peacock twenty years after he began his literary career, but because of the history of the dialogues themselves. They were contributed to the *Graphic* in five installments between the end of December 1872 and February 1873. Meredith refers to them once in a letter to Frederick Greenwood, where he says: "I am having some fun in *The Graphic* and might by and by turn the Dialogues to good purpose."[50] The venture, however, was unsuccessful;

---

[46] *Beauchamp's Career*, Vol. 11, Ch. XVII, p. 169.
[47] *Up to Midnight*, Boston, 1913.
[48] *One of Our Conquerors*, Vol. 17, Ch. V, pp. 36–41. *Ibid.*, Ch. XIX, pp. 216–221.
[49] *Gryll Grange*, Ch. XXVIII, pp. 213–226.
[50] *Letters*, Vol. 28, I, p. 239.

the dialogues are indeed dull, and the series was brought to a sudden close. As the articles had been unsigned they were speedily forgotten, escaping the notice even of the bibliographer until in 1913 a correspondent (J. D. H.) first called attention to them in *Notes and Queries*, pointing out their resemblance to the dialogues of Peacock.[51] It was then that the *Graphic* began to reprint them (February 1 and February 8, 1913). "Then Meredith's representatives suddenly discovered that there was a value in the articles, which they had apparently forgotten. Accordingly, the executors of the trustees challenged the right of the *Graphic* to publish the series again, and that journal desisted, after giving some financial solace."[52] In that same year the articles appeared in book form; and so a lost Meredith item was given once more, complete, to the world.

He, however, who seeks out the *Up to Midnight* series of *causeries* with high expectation of regalement by scintillant wit, is bound to be disappointed. The series is deadly reading, and is interesting only in an archaeological way. The issues that it treats of are gone; the humor is fumbling and heavy-labored. Its chief interest lies in the close imitation it offers of Peacock's method, and the attempt made by Meredith to catch his style and spirit. But the book is only the dry bones of Peacock; Meredith, as has been pointed out elsewhere, never could reproduce successfully the peculiar turn of Peacock's ironic style; when he follows him most closely, he fails most conspicuously. And so it is in *Up to Midnight*. If, however, Peacock's informing spirit escapes Meredith, it is not for lack of attention to the Peacockian formulae. These Meredith has followed strictly. In fact, Meredith has taken for his model Peacock's earliest book, *Headlong Hall*, and reproduced its situation and characters, not only in their types but in the very method of their naming. The controversy is of the same heated kind that passes between the *personae* of *Headlong Hall;* for every subject attempted there

---

[51] *Notes and Queries*, 11 S VII, Jan. 18, 1913; *Ibid.*, 11 S X, Sept. 21, 1919. See also for the same matter: Chislett, Wm., Jr., *George Meredith, A Study and Appraisal*, Boston, 1923.
[52] *Note* inside the cover of the British Museum copy of *Up to Midnight*, signed *J. M. Bullock*.

is the Yea and the Nay; with the rest of the company for arbitrators. Only the subject matter is changed; and this with Meredith consists, as was perhaps dictated by his writing for a public print, of items of current interest: the Alabama Claims, Stanley's rescue expedition, the latest attempt to reach the Pole, and the raising of the French indemnity loan. Over such points of interest controversy can scarcely furiously rage, even when they are fresh; they do not cut deep enough into the prejudices of men to bring out passionate pronouncements. And, indeed, it is perhaps for this reason as much as any that Meredith's *causeries* fall flat. Peacock, more wisely, except for a few pet aversions, such for example as his dislike for paper currency, which he conceived as a fraud and cheat, never wrought his dialogue out of purely contemporary matter. His interests were of a more general sort, affecting basic matters; and, therefore, capable of a more stirring presentation. From such topics Meredith's task as journalist naturally debarred him; accordingly, his work suffers.

However, in its scheme, Meredith's work is pure Peacock. For Squire Headlong we have substituted Sir John Saxon; and for Headlong Hall, a spacious house at Alley-in-Arden, Warwickshire. The scene has shifted from Wales into England, but the change is comparatively unimportant when the similarities of the general situation are considered. There is the same gathering at the Christmas season as in Peacock; the same sitting at table; the same evenings in the drawing-room. The characters, likewise, resemble Peacock's company: there is the unwearied optimist, Mr. Brighton, and the consistent pessimist, Mr. Finestare; who correspond to Peacock's Mr. Foster and Mr. Escot. Sir Patrick, another of the characters, suggests Mr. Patrick O'Prism, Peacock's Irishman. Mr. Helion and Mr. M'Nimbis, by their names at least, for their characters are not clearly drawn, suggest Peacock's classically named people. At all points, then, the analogy holds; as an example of work formulated on the model of a definite original, the origins of *Up to Midnight* are clear.

Equally sure in its source is Meredith's fantastic interlude,

The Rajah in London,[53], which he introduces in *One of Our Conquerors* as "that nationally interesting Poem, or Dramatic Satire, once famous," for which he playfully gives the reference: "London, Limbo and Sons, 1889." Just as Peacock had raised from the dead spirits of the ancient world to laugh at modern London, so does Meredith, with a change of persons, bring a Rajah and his Minister from the East to wonder at the ways of the City. The idea is, beyond doubt, taken from Peacock, from Peacock's latest novel, as is clearly indicated not only in the nature of the episode, but by the title, which is Peacock's except that the name *Rajah* is substituted for *Aristophanes*. To Meredith, however, must be given credit for the more artistic conception and more skillful handling of the idea. Not only is a concretely picturesque figure drawn in place of Peacock's fleeting shade; but a sense of wonder and perplexity in the mind of the Rajah supplants the curtness and final mockery of Peacock's visitors. Playing with this idea of a stranger in England, an old notion that Peacock had thrice introduced,[54] Meredith gives it a new value, and even something of a poetic flavor. The intention of the piece is the same as Peacock's: satire, but the means are more adroit. For example, the conclusion of the Indians, drawn from their observation of the tides of London traffic, that the English are really Zoroastrians: "worshipping, they march Eastward at morn, Westward at eve. For that way lies the key, this way the cupboard, of the supplies, their fuel," provides not only a vivid, picturesque image, but a criticism that penetrates subtly, under cover of a figure, to the master-motive of English life. Likewise, when we are told that the Rajah and his Minister enter a Gin-Palace "to witness a service that they have learned to observe as Anglicanly religious," it is the same delightful incongruity between things said and things meant that gives the satire its effect. Here, although Meredith is following Peacock very definitely, he shows himself the more ingenious and powerful

---

[53] *One of Our Conquerors*, Vol. 17, Ch. V, pp. 36–41.
[54] Calidore of the fragmentary novel of that name and the Jupiter of the *Aristophanes in London* passage of *Gryll Grange* have already been mentioned as examples of wandering strangers marvelling at the spectacle of England. To these Sir Oran Haut-ton of *Melincourt* must surely be added.

satirist; the merely clumsy strength of Peacock is replaced by a playful spirit that lightens all it touches.

Less fortunate, however, in its effect is the Delphica episode, which also draws a broken length through *One of Our Conquerors*.[55] It is reported as the composition of Colney Durance, the splenetic national critic; by title it is called a *Satiric Serial Tale;* and we are told it is "matter for an Epic." In brief, the narrative relates the expedition of the Rev. Dr. Bouthain and his curate, the Rev. Mr. Semhians, to the court of Japan to plead the superior merits of the English language against the other tongues of Europe. It is a situation fraught with keen competition; for Germany, France, Russia, and even Greece have representatives to plead their claims. The point of the satire is to show how the English are crippled in rivalry with other people, by their self-complacency, their reliance on past successes and on destiny. Against an aggressive Germany, represented by Dr. Gannius and his smiling daughter Delphica, and against an ambitious America well-furnished with money, England is shown as almost powerless.

As satire the *Serial Tale* makes its point, but the whole business is wearisomely dull, and is an excrescence upon the book into which it is thrust. Undoubtedly it derives from Peacock in two particulars. In the first place, it is a simple reversal of the old theme, before mentioned, of the innocent stranger come among the English: instead it shows the Englishman, provincial and self-satisfied, turned loose in foreign parts. The second Peacockian element consists of the gathering together of the rival national representatives aboard ship, where they are forced into company and conflict. The assembly of Dr. Bouthoin, Dr. Gannius, M. Falarique, M. Bobinikine and M. Mytharetes constitutes a Peacockian group. It suggests the embattled table-companies of *Headlong Hall* or *Crochet Castle*, which, undoubtedly, are its antecendents. Delphica, too, the heroine, fair and troubling daughter of a learned father, reminds one of Miss Cephalia Cranium, daughter of the learned phrenologist of *Headlong Hall;* her ability to win favor for her father's cause

---

[55] *One of Our Conquerors*, Vol. 17, Ch. XIX, pp. 216–221.

suggests the analogy. The elements of Peacock, as in the *Up to Midnight* dialogues, are here unquestionably. And, in this particular phantasy, as in those dialogues, Meredith is adopting Peacockian formulae for extending comment upon contemporary tendencies in English life. It is significant that both these efforts are artistically unsuccessful. Only in the brief *Rajah in London* phantasy does Meredith use Peacock's technique successfully; and in that instance he transcends it by a brilliant *tour de force*. There was a quickness in Meredith's wit which put him at a disadvantage in copying Peacock at length. It is characteristic that when he does so, he falls below the level of the lesser man. That he did so, in an imitative effort, cannot be denied.

VI

The Dinner Table and Afterward

One of the most conspicuous features of Meredith's writing, undoubtedly, is the deliberate manner in which he has chosen to delineate a single stratum of society. His people, on the whole, are from the top of society; these are his chosen group, for whom as it were, he is willing to sacrifice the rest. Of course, an occasional figure may intrude upon the scene from outside these arbitrary limits; an Evan Harrington working his way up to a higher station from humble beginnings; or, conversely, a Princess Ottilia temporarily descending from her royal seat to love a commoner; but these are the exceptions; and in either case it is the ascension or declension of the individual into a social atmosphere hostile or foreign to him, that provides the basic situation of the story. Still, simply to group Meredith's people under the broad heading "aristrocatic" is to furnish a very inadequate notion of them, for they are essentially a peculiar people, a very special group among the larger group to whom that term is usually applied. In fact, they belong to their class only in respect to their possession of a degree of wealth, and the enjoyment of such station and means of ease as wealth brings. Their importance as successful business men, their influence as country gentry, or their prestige of title or noble connection has little to do with Meredith's interest in them; for Meredith's concern is with their inward lives, not the outward circumstance of their existence.

However, because wealth and station give to their happy possessors the best opportunities for living, for the fullest development of the senses and the mind, and make possible the most exquisite refinement of manners, it happens that Meredith's chosen people must almost necessarily be of the economically independent. But, within it, they are a world to themselves. They are the few to whom life veritably has become a fine art. It is in this sense that they constitute a select and elect society. Free from the harsh necessity of toil which binds most humanity, they use their leisure in perfecting the amenities of social intercourse. Indeed, it is the stress placed upon the social ideal that makes these people, so ineffectual as judged by any practical standards, so artificial as judged by their exemption from the lot of common men, remarkable; and redeems them from the stigma that attaches to idlers. In their distinctive manner really they are artists, engaged in a most difficult work, the construction of a social *milieu*. Their quest is to realize a society where men and women, blending and harmonizing their interests, may meet to their mutual satisfaction. This happy condition, so imperfectly realized in actual life but fondly glimpsed by Meredith as a possibility and described by him, is the central idea of his social portraiture. Into the mouths of his characters on occasion he puts expressions that make clear this idea. When, for example, Willoughby Patterne, speaking for himself, says that "the art is to associate a group of sympathetic friends in our neighborhood,"[1] he is simply giving expression to Meredith's grand idea. Likewise, when in *Sandra Belloni* we are bade admire Lady Gosstre's "practiced play upon the social instrument, surely the grandest of all, the chords being men and women,"[2] and are further told to "consider what an accomplishment this is," we realize that we have to do with one of Meredith's shaping sentiments.

But this social conception, so basic in Meredith as to underlie practically the whole body of his work, seems in no original sense to be Meredith's own. Rather does it seem like simply another of the inheritances which he received from the tutelage of Peacock. Peacock's use of the same leisured class, and the terms of their association, is exactly equivalent to that of Meredith. In Peacock there is found exactly the same social amalgam of wealth, the gentry, and the aristocracy that shines from Meredith's pages. And likewise in Peacock, their riches are the least of these characters' adornments; rather, there too, it is their social qualities—the intellectual interests engrafted on gentle manners, that are put forward. The ideal of a social group as a sort of symphony which becomes explicit in Meredith, is

---

[1] *The Egoist*, Vol. 13, Ch. XIII, p. 146.
[2] *Sandra Belloni*, Vol. 3, Ch. X, p. 86.

in Peacock as such unexpressed, but the behavior of the characters themselves illustrates it abundantly. It is characteristic that what Peacock might write of through arbitrary choice, Meredith, following in his steps, would justify in terms of philosophical truth. Conceivably, Peacock wrote of easy-lived society because he liked that sort of people, because he knew them, because, as one of them himself, it was his pleasure to write of them. But with Meredith, it is different: the conditions of his fiction are fixed not by whim, but by their appropriateness as means to what he desired to achieve. Accordingly, when he followed Peacock into a social realm almost unique in its structure and purposes, one may be sure he did so from no mere liking, although affinity of temperament, as with Peacock, must be allowed a factor; but for well-considered reasons of the suitability of the vehicle.

The ultimate suitability of Peacock's type of society for Meredith, as a writer, lay in its possibilities as a theatre of intellectual comedy. It is noteworthy that Meredith's people, no more than Peacock's, are represented as especially strong in the formal parts of education. The savants who are introduced from time to time muster the intellectual guns, it is true, but the central characters are more notable for intellectual nimbleness than for learning. It is in their readiness at repartee, their love of all sorts of amiable intellectual jousting, in short their gift of wit that these people are distinguished. Peacock for the purpose of his somewhat heavy controversy had created a society whose accent was on the things of the mind. It was this society with all its properties that Meredith appropriated; only Meredith altered in some degree its tone, paradoxically, both, at once, enlivening and sobering it. Meredith brightened the intellectual vistas, by substituting a flashing wit for the recital of dull fact; and sobered it by eliminating the element of horseplay wherewith Peacock had endeavored to correct heaviness of the argumentation.

In making these changes so necessary to his art, Meredith gave a new brilliance to the social scene Peacock had invented; but its properties he altered not all. Indeed, if Meredith's society be compared with Peacock's, at practically all points, a remarkable correspondence is discovered. Feature after feature in Meredith's social scene suggests an antecedent in Peacock. Victor Radnor's building his great house at Lakelands, or the Pole sisters' planning the purchase of Besworth, "a house where all the chief celebrities might be encountered," immediately recalls the social ambitions and program of Mr. Crotchet of *Crotchet Castle*.[3] The description that Meredith gives of Brookfield's proposed society exactly answers to the society of almost any Peacock novel from *Headlong Hall* down to *Gryll Grange:*[4] "the circle . . . was of this receipt: celebrities, London residents and County notables, all in their severally due proportions down, to meet, mix, and revolve: the Celebrities to shine; the Metropolitans to act as satellites; the County ignoramuses to feel flattered in knowing that all stood forth for their amusement." The country-house in Meredith as in Peacock is usually accessible from London, so that there may be "rapid relays of guests." An exception to this rule, of course, is Headlong Hall in Peacock's novel of that name. But it is especially noteworthy that the social life of Headlong Hall is reproduced in Penarvan Castle in *Sandra Belloni*,[5] with such correspondence of details as to make the identification scarcely avoidable. A Welsh castle on the night when it is filled with both English and Welsh gentry, come for the annual ball; the night cold, and the roads almost impassable: such in brief is the scene in both instances.

The recreations of Peacock's people and Meredith's, too, are surprisingly alike. There is an impulsiveness about them that, on occasion, results in most unexpected forms of entertainment. Mr. Forrester's Anti-Saccharine Festival in *Melincourt* is paralleled by Mr. Pericles' *fête champêtre* in *Sandra Belloni*.[6] But more remarkable than these monster picnics are the excursions made *en masse* by large parties of house-guests. Peacock's people are peculiarly liable to the craze. In *Melincourt* there is a coaching journey made across the length of England by the entire

---

[3] *Crotchet Castle*, Ch. I, p. 146.
[4] *Sandra Belloni*, Vol. 3, Ch. IV, p. 22.
[5] *Sandra Belloni*, Vol. 4, Ch. XLV, pp. 187–88.
[6] *Cf. Sandra Belloni*, Vol. 4, Chs. XXXI–XXXII, pp. 1–32; *Crotchet Castle*, Chs. XXVII and XXVIII, pp. 200–219.

party of characters for the purpose of seeing Sir Oran Haut-Ton elected M. P. for the town of Onevote.[7] In *Crotchet Castle*, for no reason at all, except that they desire a change of scene, the entire household of guests, upon Mr. Crotchet's invitation, departs in a fleet of boats up Thames for an extended tour into North Wales.[8] In Meredith's late novel, *One of Our Conquerors*, this sort of expedition is duplicated in the Drive to Paris, sponsored by Victor Radnor for the pleasure of himself and his friends.[9] Of the fact that the Drive is copied from Peacock's incidents of the same kind there can scarcely be doubt, it is so obvious a derivation.

The real focus of society, however, whether in Meredith or Peacock, is about the dinner table. As has been pointed out in another chapter, the people present at these gatherings are remarkably alike in both authors. To offer an example, however, there is the group at Mrs. Mountstuart's dinner in *The Egoist*.[10] The guests are true Peacockian phantasts, well assorted in regard to their manias. Among them are Mr. Capes, a governor of Bombay, who has written "a pamphlet in favor of Suttee;" Col. Wild-John, whose cry is "The Protestant Church is in danger;" and Sir Wilson Pettifer, a Monarchial-republican. Such creations are simon-pure Peacock, of course. On occasion, too, although Meredith generally makes his table-talk a battle of quick wits, a swift game of give-and-take, in which the idea passes and repasses in a variety of transformations, the conversation sometimes bears resemblance in its underlying pattern to Peacock's. For example, the luncheon in *The Egoist* where each one present around the table, in turn, attempts a definition of "a rough-truth,"[11] seems like a reflection of a similar episode in *Crochet Castle* when everyone present at dinner gives his idea for perfecting the world.[12] The difference between the situations

---

[7] *Melincourt*, Chs. XIX and XX, pp. 147–160.
[8] *Crotchet Castle*, Chs. IX and X, pp. 228–246.
[9] *One of Our Conquerors*, Vol. 17, Ch. XIV, p. 142 it seq.
[10] *The Egoist*, Vol. 14, Ch. XXVI, pp. 444–45. For the same sort of situation see also *Evan Harrington*, Vol. 6, Ch. XIV, pp. 178–79.
[11] *The Egoist*, Vol. 14, Ch. XXXVI, pp. 444–445.
[12] *Crotchet Castle*, Ch. VI, pp. 192-204.

lies simply in the brevity and trenchancy of Meredith's wit as over against Peacock's wearisome declamation. Where Meredith condenses, Peacock expands; the comparison, of course, is all in Meredith's favor. That mutuality of converse, though, that Peacock prescribed for his characters, letting each have his turn for speech, Meredith retained, as we have seen. Mrs. Mountstuart's complaint concerning Dr. Middleton's assumption of the speakership, "We seemed to have sat down to a solitary performance on the bass-viol. We were positively an assembly of insects during thunder,"[13] echoes Meredith's own feeling. His practice is always to allow utterance to all his figures; he has no dummies. In this, he is in perfect accord with Peacock.

Although both Meredith and Peacock regarded the dinner as a social occasion, they both, too, regarded it as an end in itself; and as such they have celebrated it. We are told of Gregory Gryll that "he liked to dine well, and to have quiet friends at his table with whom he could discuss questions which might afford room for pleasant conversation, and none for acrimonious dispute."[14] Such is the happy ideal of the meal with its dual functions, gastronomic and intellectual. In the praise of the food itself, however, Peacock often becomes enthusiastic to the point of extravagance. "There is but one good thing in the world, *videlicet*, a good dinner," he makes the disillusioned Mr. Glowry say in *Nightmare Abbey*.[15] In *Crotchet Castle* his ecomiums become a bit stronger still. "There is cogency in a good supper," says Dr. Folliott, who adds, most illogically, "a good dinner, in these degenerate days, bespeaks a good man."[16] For him, it is sufficient testimony of the character of a guest "that he had the good sense to bring with him a basket of lobsters." Coupled quite naturally with this love of food is the belief in its necessity for brave living, and its power as a sovereign remedy over the misfortunes of life. "Whatever happens in this world, never let it spoil your dinner," says Dr. Opimian in Peacock's last novel. This is a doctrine often insisted on in Meredith. When Adrian Harley, advising Richard, says, "Nature never forgives.

---

[13] *The Egoist*, Vol. 14, Ch. XXXIII, p. 405.
[14] *Gryll Grange*, Ch. II, p. 10.
[15] *Nightmare Abbey*, Ch. I, p. 128.
[16] *Crotchet Castle*, Ch. II, p. 154.

A lost dinner can never be replaced,"[17] the Peacockian tang of the passage forces recognition. It is the advice of Gottlieb Groschen to the Goshawk in *Farina*,[18] as also it is the word of Mrs. Harrington to her son: "Empty stomachs are poor counsellors."[19] Here undoubtedly is an echo reminiscent of Peacock's robust doctrine concerning the efficacy of good food toward right living.

The aesthetics of food likewise was a subject with which Peacock concerned himself. "There is fine music, as Rabelais observes, in the cliquetes d'assiettes, a refreshing shade in the ombre de salle a manger, and an elegant fragrance in the fumee de roti," he writes in *Crotchet Castle*.[20] The subject is resumed with greater notice in *Gryll Grange* where, beginning with the declaration, "I like to see my dinner," Dr. Opimiam speaks in favor of the old-fashioned ways of carving and serving in public.[21] The praise of the smoking coffee-urn which runs like a motif through all Peacock is another indication of the delight that the sight and sound of food held for the man. The same note of appreciation is caught in Meredith. In connection with this matter it must be remembered that his first work was a cookery book written in collaboration with his first wife, Peacock's daughter, and that he is supposed to have assisted her in writing her essay "*Gastronomy and Civilization*" for *Frazer's Magazine*.[22] But the essay also bears strong internal evidences, not only in its classical references but in its phraseology, to show that Peacock too lent his assistance in the composition.[23]

How much Meredith may have learned from Peacock in the way of a fastidious gastronomy cannot of course be determined. Perhaps, on the other hand, he brought from his own home his taste for delicate food. At any rate, his expertness in cuisine, and his appreciation of good fare remained with him a stable interest. One suspects that perhaps he became a more subtle critic of the art than Peacock himself. Peacock in several

---

[17] *Ordeal of Richard Feverel*, Vol. 6, Ch. XLIV, p. 540.
[18] *Farina*, Vol. 21, p. 30.
[19] *Evan Harrington*, Vol. 6, Ch. VII, p. 86.
[20] *Crotchet Castle*, Ch. IV, p. 175.
[21] *Gryll Grange*, Ch. XIII, pp. 87–88.
[22] Ellis, S. M., *George Meredith*, London, 1920, pp. 62–65.
[23] *Cf. Gastronomy and Civilization, Frazer's Magazine*, Dec., 1851.

places recommends cooking as one of the rudiments of a woman's training.[24] He makes Dr. Opimian furnish his cook "with the best books on cookery."[25] But there is little beside this. In fact, one imagines that Peacock cared chiefly for a substantial diet; and was not much of a hand for the rarer "kick-shaws." In contempt he makes Dr. Folliott quote a culinary authority: "Ude says an elegant supper may be given with sandwiches . . . An elegant supper! I sup when I can, but not upon sandwiches."[26] Meredith, on the other hand, seems to have demanded the greatest finesse in the art. For English cookery he had contempt: "We are further brought round to the old confession that we cannot cook." In his novels there is considerable talk of French cooks: on their skill one is made to feel the smooth functioning of the social machine depends. They truly are "a mighty necessity of the elegant." It is in regard to such food as they prepare that Meredith grows lyrical. Highly imaginative, almost poetic in tone, is the description which he gives of the great dinner at Lakelands: "every dish, one may say, advancing, curtseying, swimming to be your partner, instead of passively submitting to the eye of appetite, consenting to the teeth, as that rather melancholy procession of the cold, resembling established spinsters thrice-corseted in decorum, will appear to do."[27] This is the panegyric of food, the final word on the aesthetics of the subject. Beside such a master-stroke of sensuous analysis, Peacock's enthusiasms seem vague.

So likewise with wine, the prelude of the meal, its accompaniment, and fit conclusion: it is a subject for continual celebration by both Peacock and Meredith. Meredith's treatment of theme derives in many details directly from Peacock as will be shown. Meredith, however, characteristically treats wine as a human good, the friend of the philosophic impulse, while Peacock is likely to regard it almost wholly as a mere enlivener, the quickener of the senses, and promoter of jollity. Meredith has no lively drinking songs, such as Peacock's of the refrain:[28]

---

[24] *Gryll Grange*, Ch. XXXI, p. 247.
[25] *Ibid.*, Ch. III, p. 17.
[26] *Crotchet Castle*, Ch. II, p. 183.
[27] *One of Our Conquerors*, Vol. 17, Ch. XVII, p. 258.
[28] *Melincourt*, Ch. XVI, p. 128.

> Let the ocean be Port, and we'll think it good sport
> To be laid in that Red Sea.

Nor has he any humorous, sophistical philosophizing on the subject such as is put in the mouth of Dr. Portpipe, the disreputable clergyman of *Melincourt:* "I drink by anticipation of thirst that may be. Prevention is cure. Wine is the elixir of life. 'The soul,' says St. Augustine, 'cannot live in drought.' What is death? Dust and ashes. There is nothing so dry. What is life? Spirit. What is spirit? Wine."[29] With his deliciously faulty argument, Dr. Portpipe is worthy to stand beside Seithenyn ap Seithenyn, of the *Misfortunes of Elphin*, Peacock's most perfectly realized character, and one of the most amusing drunkards in all the range of English literature. Of this type of people Meredith has no examples.

Meredith, however, does follow Peacock in showing the lure that good wine has for a more sedate, stable type of man. The character of Dr. Middleton is in respect to this weakness is drawn evidently from Dr. Folliott, similar to him in so many points, of *Crotchet Castle*. The priority of wine in the interest of these men, even over their beloved classics, is a common bond. It was Peacock's Dr. Folliott who said "to enjoy your bottle in the present, and your book in the indefinite future, is a delightful condition of human existence,"[30] anticipating in this very succinct phrasing of wisdom, the behavior of his later counterpart, Dr. Middleton. But this is not all. In *Crotchet Castle* there is pictured a wine cellar the very likeness of the one for which Dr. Middleton was quite willing to sell his daughter. "In the cellar of my friend, Mr. Crotchet, there is the talismanic antidote (for diseases engendered by water) of a thousand dozen of old wine, a beautiful spectacle, I assure you, and a model of arrangement."[31] The resemblance to the wine-cellar of Patterne Hall is unmistakable.[32]

---

[29] *Melincourt*, Ch. XVI, pp. 121–122.
[30] *Crotchet Castle*, Ch. VII, p. 208.
[31] *Ibid.*, Ch. II, p. 157.
[32] *The Egoist*, Vol. 13, Ch. XX, p. 228.

In the picturing of post-prandial sessions over the wine, too, Meredith has given us pictures that fetch home to Peacock for their original. The meeting of the Ante-deluvians in *Evan Harrington*, for example, hearkens back to the rude hospitality of Sir Harry Headlong.[33] It is in *The Amazing Marriage*, however, that we have the best representation of a Peacockian drinking bout. The festival is the fitting hospitality extended by the English gentry to the Welshmen that have brought Carinthia up from Wales. The account of the occasion is briefly this:[34] "The united races took the table in Esslemont's dining hall for a memorable night of it. . . . Whatever happened, they sat down together, and the point of honor for them, each and every one, was not to be the first to rise from it. . . . Each English gentleman had a Welsh gentleman beside him; they both sat firm, they both fell together. The bottles they circulated to an empty glass. All drank equally. Often the voices were high, the talk was loud. The gentlemen were too serious to sing. . . . The Welsh and English gentlemen consumed the number of nine dozen and a half of old Esslemont wine before they rose or possibly sank, at the festive board at the hour of five in the morning." In all details, except that they did not sing, this account might well be an excerpt from any of Peacock's earlier novels. The mingling of Celt and Saxon suggests particularly the hospitality of *Headlong Hall*. The perpetually filled glass recalls Sir Harry's jovial cry, "No heel-taps, here!" Both in business and spirit it is Peacock done again.

Not always though do "the rays of the midnight lamp tremble over many a lengthening file of empty bottles." More often, even in Peacock, the occasion is decorous, and of that sort of meeting the examples in Meredith are more numerous. At such times, the appreciation of the delicate palate finds expression. How often in Peacock acrimonious debate is lulled by a tribute to the wine: "Before I proceed with this discussion—Vin or Grave, Mr. Skionar?" "Sir, I must drown my inadvertence in a glass of Sauterne with you."[35] Such are the tactful uses of the

---

[33] *Evan Harrington*, Vol. 6, Ch. XII, pp. 132-144.
[34] *The Amazing Marriage*, Vol. 19, Ch. XXXIV, pp. 354-55.
[35] *Crotchet Castle*, Ch. IV, p. 179.

wine in the etiquette of Dr. Folliott; and his wont in this respect gives the tone of Peacock's amenable tables. It is in terms of such diplomatic and appreciative usage that Meredith introduces wine in his pages. The mixed monologue lingers in them. When, in *One of Our Conquerors*, Simeon Fenellan reports to Radnor, "I have dined with Mr. Carling:—capital claret,"[36] we catch the very accent of Dr. Folliott's table talk; the same confusion of serious discussion with impulsive tribute to the God.

It is in the same book that Meredith puts his greatest tribute to wine, in a long passage of lyrical tone. The occasion is the opening of a bottle of Old Veuve, "a champagne of a sobered sweetness, of a great year, a great age, counting up to the extremer maturity attained by wines of stilly depths; and thus worthy comrade despite the wanton sparkles, for the promoting of the state of reverential wonderment in rapture, which an ancient wine will lead to, well you wot."[36] Then follows the body of the dithyramb. "The silly, girly, sugary crudity has given way to womanly suavity, matronly composure, with yet the sparkles; they ascend; but the hue and flavour tell of a soul that has come to lodgement there. It conducts the youthful man to temples of dusky thought: philosophers partaking of it are drawn by the arms of garlanded nymphs about their necks into the fathomless of inquiries." It is in this aspect, as to a humanizing agent, that Meredith gives his final benediction to the grape. Wine, he says, like music, is an agent to "bring out the native bent of the civilized man: endue him with language, too;" again "that the Bacchus of a suspicious birth induces ever to the worship of the loftier Deities." This is the philosophy of Peacock, but raised to a loftier plane, and expressed with a delicacy of feeling foreign to Peacock. Again in this is Meredith the refiner of theme and material.

In both Peacock and Meredith music is introduced as an additional instrument of social harmony. The people of Peacock's novels are all strongly musical; the heroines all play and sing, and usually there is a professional musician in the company

---

[36] *One of Our Conquerors*, Vol. 17, Ch. VIII, p. 129.
[37] *One of Our Conquerors*, Vol. 17, Ch. III, pp. 17–18.

who acts at once as a comic figure and the promoter of musical programs. "Music and conversation," writes Peacock of the life at Melincourt, "consumed the evenings."[38] The description is typical of his evenings, and might easily be applied to Meredith's as well. It was Victor Radnor of *One of Our Conquerors* who discovered of his guests that "music harmonized them." The small orchestra which he organized among his friends was the bond that united an ill-assorted group of otherwise uncongenial oddities.[39] Their first public performance was one of the features of the opening of the great house at Lakelands.[40] A parallel to this sort of amateur effort, it will be remembered, is given by Peacock in *Gryll Grange*, where the music and chorus singing of the masque *Aristophanes in London* is all given by the guests at the Grange.[41] Other parallels of a striking sort in connection with musical activities exist between Peacock and Meredith. Tracy Runningbrook, writing an opera libretto for Sandra Belloni,[42] suggests Mr. Trillo's composition of an opera at Crotchet Castle. The comparison is heightened by the knowledge that Mr. Trillo "took the opinion of the young ladies on every step in its progress; occasionally regaling the company with specimens."[42] He too, in the light of his declared belief, prompts the idea that Mr. Antonio Pericles, the musical impresario and fantastic, that concerned himself so about Sandra, inherited, in part, from him. Mr. Trillo's obsession was, briefly, "that an opera in perfection was . . . the most efficient instrument of civilization;" it is a fixed idea sufficiently like Mr. Pericles' excessive value of a golden voice, at least, to warrant the comparison.[43] Meredith's love of the opera was highly developed; references to the older Italian operas, for whose tuneful melodies he had a predilection, although a little ashamed of it, and to Wagner run through the novels. In comparison with Peacock, whose simpler taste seems to have inclined to balladry, his knowledge and appreciation of music must have been infinitely

---

[40] *One of Our Conquerors*, Vol. 17, Ch. XX, p. 237.
[41] *Gryll Grange*, Ch. XXVIII, p. 213 et seq.
[42] *Sandra Belloni*, Vol. 3, Ch. XXIII, pp. 223–27.
[43] *Cf. Crotchet Castle*, Ch. X, p. 240; *Sandra Belloni*, Vol. 3, Ch. I, pp. 2–4

greater. In the social application of music, and in his manifest borrowing of incidents, however, he follows Peacock. It is a part of that social atmosphere which, as a whole, Peacock created and which Meredith, although with variations and improvements, reproduced in all its major features.

In setting out this picture of social life, Meredith was representing an ideal which, as he knew, was scarcely realized at all in the England of his day. Writing to Maxse, he asks, "Your evenings—but what are an Englishman's evenings?" To the rhetorical question he supplies a ready answer. "Hot-beds of dyspepsia as a rule. There should be liveliness, music, billiards, dancing, dialogue, laughter—choice of all these. Instead of which—I ask you!"[44] It is appropriate that the items of his list should be the elements that make festive the social scene of his novels. But the list too is a perfect epitome of Peacock's *milieu* as well. The correspondence is point for point. Perhaps from his life under Peacock's roof, certainly from his books, Meredith gained an ideal of social urbanity. Scarcely could he have acquired it earlier in a provincial town, in a tradesman's home, no matter how socially aspiring the family. Neither does it come of schools. But once acquired it was his forever. In one respect it may be regarded as an integral part of the propaganda, the teaching of a more intellectual and happy life; in another, the necessity of his art, the fixed conditions under which his social comedy could come into being. In its features the scheme is Peacock's, but Meredith the borrower, here, becomes its perfecter and justifier. What in Peacock was crude and pointless, becomes with Meredith an artistic vehicle of a unique sort. It may be said truly that if Meredith had not known the prototype of such a society, he would have been compelled to invent it. Fortunately, ready-made, it came to his hand. That he realized the fitness of Peacock's society for his purpose is another mark of his keen perception of the possibilities of things, and of his power of adaptation.

---

[44] *Letters*, Vol. 28, I, p. 102.

VII

Woman

In no other department of thought do Meredith and Peacock show a closer agreement than in regard to woman and the necessity of her intellectual and emotional emancipation. Meredith, perhaps because he lived on into a period when woman was achieving a new status, has made more particular suggestions for her welfare: commending her entrance into politics and the professions, both for her own good and the nation's. Moreover, because the agitation for women's rights was gathering head in his time, Meredith by his fearless espousing of woman's cause has obtained the honor belonging to a chivalric spokesman. Of Peacock's feminism, on the other hand, little is heard, not because he spoke less vigorously than Meredith on the subject, but because he spoke out of time. Meredith too spoke, in a sense, out of time; but although Meredith in championing woman was anticipating his age, writing for our time rather than his own, nevertheless he did not completely outrun it. There was even then a minority body of opinion to applaud and second his efforts. Peacock, in his day, had stood comparatively alone. A survey of the novel contemporary of his own time, the novel of Miss Austen, Miss Edgeworth, and Sir Walter Scott, shows nothing comparable to the self-sufficient women of Peacock's fiction. The honor then must be allowed Peacock of being one of the first, and certainly one of the most vigorous of the champions of free womanhood. Whereas Meredith wrote on the threshold of a period of social change, Peacock wrote in a time when as yet any large alteration in the status of the sexes could scarcely be expected. The changes that were working in industry and politics must, of course, eventually have resulted in a breakdown of the old rule; but in Peacock's day the traditional social structure, so far as the manners, education, and relations of the sexes were concerned, stood firm.

Therefore it is surprising how audaciously modern the majority of his female characters are. Their resemblance to the young goddesses of Meredith's novels is in many points striking. Moreover, in their point of view both novelists show a remarkable coincidence. This situation is, however, the less surprising when it is considered how sane and liberal Peacock's position in regard to woman really is. He marked in their out-line all the claims for woman which later feminists could possibly assert for the sex; in the nature of things, it was scarcely possible for Meredith to enlarge upon his father-in-law's genuine and humane philosophy of the subject. But, as has been said before, the resemblance between them both in general attitude toward the subject, and the presentation of particular phases of it, is such as to suggest that here is another point of intellectual contact between the two, whereby the shrewd insight of the elder man was brought to fertilize the genius of the younger. Undoubtedly Meredith's interest which led him to observe women so closely and to analyze them so minutely yet lovingly, was an original force of his nature that needed no external prompting to arouse or direct it. That Meredith would have written much of women under any circumstances may be assumed without question. Nevertheless, that he was helped to a definite, rational philosophy toward women under the tutelage of his father-in-law seems probable and demonstrable. Their attitudes are too much alike all around to be merely fortuitous agreement.

Peacock, viewing the position of woman in his earlier day, saw her crippled chiefly by two considerations: first, the mercenary terms dictating her marriage; and, second, that faulty education which limited her intellectual growth and repressed her healthy emotions. The problem of woman's place in society Peacock first broached seriously in *Melincourt*, where in the person of Anthelia Melincourt, the heroine, he traced in detail the portrait of his feminine ideal. The circumstances of this girl's rearing, the reader is told, were most unusual, for her father, Sir Henry Melincourt, "devoted himself in solitude to the cultivation of his daughter's understanding; for he was one of those who maintained the heretical notion that women are, or at least may be, rational beings . . . though from the pains usually taken in what is called education, to make them otherwise, there are few examples to warrant the truth of the theory."[1] It is in this same novel that Peacock, regarding the more usual manner of women's training, asks: "If women are to be treated only as pretty dolls, and dressed in all the fripperies of irrational education . . . is it to be inferred that they are incapable of better things?"[2] This same comparison of woman with a doll appears also in Peacock's following novel, *Nightmare Abbey*, where he makes Scythrop, his hero, remark, "But how is it that their minds are locked up? The fault is in their artificial education which studiously models them into mere musical dolls, to be set out for sale in the great toyshop of society."[3] This assumption of Peacock's that woman's inferiority arises chiefly from her limited and faulty education, becomes in later years Meredith's own. Both men make the same diagnosis and prescribe the same cure for a patent evil. Meredith writes in like vein, "I have been oppressed by the injustice done to women, the constraint put upon their natural aptitudes and faculties, generally much to the degradation of the race. . . . They will so educate their daughters that they will not be instructed to think themselves naturally inferior to men."[4]

Being so agreed in their premises, it is not surprising that in their general conclusions on the subject Meredith and Peacock should be in almost perfect harmony. The education they both alike recommend for women is no simple training, but a broad humane education including scholarly, social, and even athletic accomplishments. Woman, perfected in mind, body, and spirit, is their common ideal, even as it is theirs for men. But basic to all progress in this direction is the necessity for women to think. "I can foresee great and blessed changes for the race when they [women] have achieved independence; for that must come of the exercise of their minds," writes Meredith.[5] In this pronouncement one catches view of that same general situation that made Anthelia, the enlightened heroine of *Melincourt*, exclaim, "To

---

[1] *Melincourt*, Ch. I, p. 9.
[2] *Melincourt*, Ch. XV, p. 117.
[3] *Nightmare Abbey*, Ch. I, p. 131.
[4] *Letters*, Vol. 29, II, 562.
[5] *Letters*, Vol. 29, II, 419.

think is one of the most unpardonable errors a woman can commit in the eyes of society. In our society a taste for intellectual pleasures is almost equivalent to taking the veil."⁶ Anthelia in this plaint suggests the plight of her spiritual sisters, later born but of the same temper, of Meredith's Princess Ottilia, "a woman who could only love intelligently," and of Clara Middleton, whose dreadful sense of isolation is derived from her willfulness in thinking for herself.

Although Peacock kindly provides for his lonely Anthelia a mate in Mr. Forester, "who can justly appreciate that most heavenly of earthly things, an enlightened female mind,"⁷ it is apparent that Peacock was fully aware of the problem created for his thinking woman in a society unused to her kind. She in turn necessarily must have a thinking mate; and thinking men, as Peacock indicates, are scarcely more plentiful than thoughtful women. Indeed, with the exception of *Nightmare Abbey*, all of Peacock's novels have as their central interest the love-match of an intellectual woman with an intellectual man, both of whom prior to their meeting have lived more or less alone, unable to find in the society of either sex a worthy companionship. Peacock, however, is ever kind to his people; his romances are a kind of miracle whereby a happy but unlikely consummation is brought about.

It is this mutuality of interest, this compatibility of temperament, that Peacock establishes as the foundation of true marriage and that Meredith after him proclaims in even less mistakable fashion. Even in his first novel, *Headlong Hall*, Peacock had set forth the doctrine, paradoxically enough, by the lips of Mr. Escot, the Deteriorationist: "The affection of two congenial spirits, united not by legal bondage and superstitious imposture, but by mutual confidence and reciprocal virtues, is the only counter-balancing consolation in this scene of mischief and misery."⁸ In *Melincourt* the same opinion is expressed by the wise Anthelia, "that mutual knowledge of each other's tastes, feelings, and character (are) I should think the only sure bases of

---

⁶ *Melincourt*, Ch. XV, pp. 117–118.
⁷ *Ibid*.
⁸ *Headlong Hall*, Ch. XV, p. 122.

matrimonial happiness."[9] It is interesting that Anthelia gives her definition apropos of expressing a doubt of the lasting felicity of marriages hastily undertaken. In Peacock affection is always shown growing by slow stages; the attachment ripens through a process of mutual observation long drawn out. There is, of course, the element of liking at first sight, but confirmation usually comes only after dubitative pausings that Peacock makes matter for humor. The resemblance in this regard to Meredith is striking. Predicating true affection on a complex harmony of physical, mental, and psychical elements, Meredith often bids his reader be patient as his characters tarry uncertain. It takes a long while for Harry Richmond to discover his true mate close at home; it takes time for Diana to realize the fineness of faithful Redworth. Likewise Vittoria learns the worth of Powys only after wanderings elsewhere. Beauchamp, poor fellow, misses his mate altogether; Aminta retrieves at cost her false step; Fleetwood makes his discovery too late, past all retrieval. Both novelists are agreed on the terms of true union, and the hazards with which it is to be achieved. Peacock, with his love of paradox, has put the difficulty in the words with which Forrester compliments his Anthelia:[10] "The only mind that can deserve to love you is the one that would never have known love if it had never known you." This saying is perhaps more distinguished for its point than its absolute truth; yet it sums up the problem. Meredith, of course, while not admitting the exclusiveness of love, or the uniqueness of its possibility in connection with given persons, does subscribe to the seriousness and chance of the quest. His novels, indeed, are but lengthy expositions of the difficulty.

The foremost trait, perhaps, both of Peacock's and Meredith's women, is their independence in ordering their lives, to which, as necessary corollaries, a certain unconventionality of manner, and a frank admission of their attachments must be added. The character of Stella in *Nightmare Abbey* is the first of Peacock's rather unconventional females. Discovered by Scythrop in his

---

[9] *Melincourt*, Ch. II, p. 19.
[10] *Melincourt*, Ch. XX, p. 159.

own apartment, she says ironically, concerning their meeting, "If you had met me in a drawing-room, and I had been introduced to you by an old woman, it would have been a matter of course."[11] Presently she tells more of herself. "I submit not to be an accomplice in my sex's slavery. . . . I rely on myself; I act as I please, go where I please, and let the world say what it will." Concerning a husband she says, "that she should take the liberty to choose for herself." And finally, "If I ever love," says she, "I shall do so without restriction or limits." Such are a few of the declarations of this young revolutionary, who apparently has tossed all decorum to the winds. Her very hiding in the Abbey, it must be remembered, is the result of her fleeing from her father, who has determined a marriage for her. In all these sentiments, however, she is justified by Peacock; he shows her as no mad-cap, but as a resolute young woman merely claiming the right over her own life. Of a less melodramatic sort is Anthelia, the heroine of *Melincourt*. She shares with Morgana of *Gryll Grange* the honors as Peacock's most carefully delineated woman. Really she is an exhibit, carefully contrived to show all the beauties of the more natural, yet more cultivated type of woman. She is in a very real sense an exemplar. When abducted by the beastly Lord Anophel, she defies him to dishonor her, saying, "I know too well the difference between the true quality of a pure and simple mind and the false affected modesty that goes by that name in the world to be intimidated by threats which can only be dictated by this supposition that your wickedness would be my disgrace, and that false shame would induce me to conceal what both truth and justice would command me to make known."[12] In regard to Forrester, her accepted lover, her frankness is equal. We are told that "she did not dissemble to herself that their interest was reciprocal;"[13] again, that she clung "to the arm of her lover not with a light and scarcely perceptible touch, but with a cordial and unsophisticated pressure."[14] In such manner does Anthelia flout all the conventional ideals of female timidity and humility. Boldest of all, however, is Morgana

---
[11] *Nightmare Abbey*, Ch. X, pp. 203–05.
[12] *Melincourt*, Ch. XLII, p. 319.
[13] *Melincourt*, Ch. XIX, p. 147.

Gryll, rebuking Lord Curryfin who has indiscreetly paid her suit while his affections were held elsewhere. Her speech on the occasion is memorable: "You offered yourself to me, to have and to hold, forever and aye. Suppose I claim you. Do not look so frightened. You deserve some punishment, but that would be too severe. . . . You must be aware that you are a great criminal; and you have not a word to say in your own justification."[14] Able to dispose not only of Curryfin, she addresses the hesitating Falconer, whom she loves, giving him one month in which to determine upon a proposal.[15] In Morgana the customary rôles of the sexes are for the moment reversed; she is nothing if not commonsense and efficient. It is remarkable too that Miss Niphet, Morgana's friend, when she at last receives the mortified but relieved Curryfin's proposal, accepts him, saying that she has longed for the occasion and then pausing, asks, "Am I too frank for you?" From these illustrations perhaps an adequate idea of the Peacockian woman can be obtained. In spirit she is intrepid, she owns no sense of inferiority to any man whatever, and manages her affairs in accordance with the joint counsel of her heart and head. The majesty, so proper to Meredith's woman, is in her, and, what is more, something of hardness which Meredith wisely subtracts from his creations.

The analogues of these feminine innovators, of course, are common enough in Meredith. We meet them there without surprise, and yet we should, for their likes are not more common in the fiction of Meredith's contemporaries than in that of Peacock's. Indeed, only in Peacock can we see their anticipated image; and it is for that reason the notion of an infiltrating influence is scarcely escapable. The unabashed love of Rose Jocelyn for Evan Harrington is an early example of the emergence of the type in Meredith's work. When reminded by her aunt of the genteel code for young women, Rose balks at advice, saying in fashion reminiscent of Peacock's heroines, "And ought I to look under my eyes, and blink and shrink whenever I come near a gentleman?"[16] We are told, too, of the rebellious girl, that it

---

[14] *Gryll Grange*, Ch. XXIV, pp. 188–196.
[15] *Gryll Grange*, Ch. XXX, p. 240.
[16] *Evan Harrington*, Vol. 6, Ch. XXXVII, p. 346.

was her misfortune to be able to love only where her mind led her, another definitely Peacock characteristic. Meredith continues his line of frankly loving girls in Sandra Belloni, whose chief offense, not only to the easily scandalized Pole sisters and conventional Georgiana Ford, but to Wilfred Pole himself, is her freely expressive nature, her complete lack of inhibiting manners.[17] To this group too belongs the Princess Ottilia, ready to sacrifice a kingdom for her love, and the awakened Cecelia Halkett ready to plunge with her lover.

In Clara Middleton we have portrayed with great detail the difficulties which stand in the way of a woman, no matter how clear-eyed, when she attempts to break the shackles society has imposed upon her. Indeed, it may be remarked, perhaps the chief difference between Peacock's treatment of woman's problem and Meredith's is that Peacock's women are always favored by special circumstances with a complete enfranchisement that allows them without opposition to dictate terms to society and follow their inclinations with relatively faint criticism. Meredith, conversely, as the artist with his eye on reality, gives his heroines no special protection or immunity, but involves them in a battle for their freedom. Accordingly, we have Cecelia Hackett, struggling against her family and her education, seemingly deserted by her lover; Clara Middleton, fighting against parental and social odds, with comparatively little help beside is her own timid, half-formed resolution; Diana, a free spirit, making room for herself in a hostile society, until she sinks in exhaustion. Indeed, only in the figure of Carinthia of *The Amazing Marriage* has Meredith created a heroine utterly self-resolute and complete after the fashion of Peacock. Under persecution, Carinthia, like Anthelia, does not bend but grows stronger; her treatment of Fleetwood echoes Morgana Gryll's dismissal of Lord Curryfin. She alone is equal to her fate by inherent force of nature.

A second point of similarity between Peacock's and Meredith's women is in the likeness of their intellectual training. It is a training which, in the first place, in the words of the idealistic

---

[17] Sandra like Peacock's Anthelia proposes: *Sandra Belloni*, Vol. 3, Ch. XX, p. 197.

Beauchamp, is "to teach them to rely upon themselves." In the second place, it is continuous, not stopping with marriage, but keeping on through the years.[18] In *One of Our Conquerors*, Meredith explains the necessity for this: to the advantage both of the woman herself and of the man. In the first instance, it is morally wrong to require of woman "a surrender of her faculties to his (man's) greater powers, such as no soul of breathing body should yield to man, not to the highest, not to the Titan, not to the most god-like of men." "Under cloak they demand it," adds Meredith, "they demand their bane."[19] And the bane is that with an untrained mate men "have but half the woman to go through life with," the physical woman, the intellectual being extinguished.[20] These words of active propaganda and of caution, just quoted, are, of course, all Meredith's, who was ever conscious that "the very smallest between nuptial lovers is a division—and that may become a mortal wound to their one life."[21] It is because Meredith is dealing with an imperfect humanity that his words of warning are necessary; but to Peacock, who deals in idealization rather than character, they are superfluous. His Anthelia and his Forrester, his Morgana and Mr. Falconer move on a level above the mere human; and one knows from their reiterated opinions that their ideas are so just, and their tempers so composed that any unjust intrusion of one upon the other is unthinkable. But these people are perfect, because they have already achieved what Meredith pleads for among ordinary humankind; by the same token they are not quite real. Peacock's people express all that he means, for they are mere types, the vehicles of a theory. Meredith, on the other hand, dealing with the realities of human nature itself, can only comment on the difficulties of his characters. But both men, independent of their individual methods, are preaching the same doctrine.

It is interesting to discover what, apart from "positive brainstuff," that is her self-reliant mode of thinking, the more formal

---

[18] *Sandra Belloni*, Vol. 3, Ch. XXII, p. 220.
[19] *One of Our Conquerors*, Vol. 17, Ch. XXV, p. 306.
[20] *Ibid.*, Ch. XXXVIII, p. 454.
[21] *Ibid.*, Ch. XIX, p. 205.

part of the education of the Peacockian and Meredithian woman consists; for in this matter of the furnishing of the mind, as on other points, our novelists are in essential agreement. In both a knowledge of languages, of the Greek and Latin, and of the modern Italian, is held basic. An acquaintance with history and philosophy derived from the languages or built upon them may be added. Science, if it be considered at all, is represented by botany, a study made practicable and appealing by the familiarity of the materials. Music too may be added as an accomplishment. But the languages remain, in all cases, the one fundamental element. It is Peacock's way however to pretend that it is the Italian rather than the classical tongues that are to be stressed in the list of feminine studies, although young women may be familiar with the latter.[22] His heroines all read Italian romances for their pleasure; in fact they dote upon them. Berni, Boriardo, and the great Ariosto with his *Orlando* are the writers whom they quote. That Peacock did not consider such imaginative literature the most healthful for woman is indicated by fact that he makes Anthelia remark that a woman may suffer from a too great idealism fostered by such reading; while Morgana, his most resolute heroine, although very fond of the Italian, is represented as a deeply-read classicist.[23] But his pretended distrust of philosophical studies for women is purely ironical. Peacock's own view, we may assume, coincides quite with that of Dr. Folliott of Crotchet Castle, who would give the full privilege of citizenship to the woman "who can construe and metricize a chorus"; just as he had reserved the privilege to those men only who had that ability.[24] Again, in Mr. Forrester's expressed desire to teach Anthelia the classic tongues, of whose literature she has been made curious by her Italian reading, we catch sight of the true Peacock.[25] He himself an admirer of the Italian, but more particularly a lover of the ancient classics, he would draw woman along the same path of studies. To the classics, the Italian, in his estimation, is but a kind of door, an easy approach

---

[22] *Melincourt*, Ch. XV, pp. 117–119.
[23] *Gryll Grange*, Ch. VI, p. 208.
[24] *Crotchet Castle*, Ch. VI, p. 202.
[25] *Melincourt*, Ch. XV, p. 151.

whereby gradually women may be lured from frivolous pursuits and profitless novel-reading into a better interest. Such evidently is his hope.

Meredith's women in their reading strikingly resemble Peacock's. Indeed, in Meredith, so far as this department is concerned, there is nothing new. When in *Richard Feverel* Lady Blandish says, "I have finished Boiardo and taken up Berni,[26]" she is simply repeating what any of Peacock's heroines might have said. When Aunt Bel in *Evan Harrington* remarks, "A young man would not marry a woman with Latin, but would not guess it the impediment,"[27] she is simply putting in another phrase the thought of Peacock's Anthelia. Likewise, when Methyr Powys in *Sandra Belloni* insists on Sandra's reading Roman history rather than her beloved Dante, one is reminded of a harsher Forrester who would force the classics on his beloved.[28] It must be remarked, too, that they read Ariosto together; an exercise out of which love may peep, as had been illustrated by the principals of *Gryll Grange* published just three years previously. The Princess Ottilia, with her specially liberal education, is the very type of Peacock's heroines.[29] Mr. Austen, in *Beauchamp's Career*, reads Roman history to Cecelia Halkett in the manner of a Peacock hero.[30] Clara Middleton, of *The Egoist*, knows both Latin and Greek, and acts to the bent of her education.[31] In *Diana of the Crossways*, Lady Dunstane reads both Latin and Greek,[32] while Diana herself, unfurnished with the older tongues, reads "books of all sorts, political, philosophical, economical, romantic." Under Redworth's tutelage she becomes a student of botany, ornithology, and astronomy.[33] From such illustrations, it must be clear how closely Meredith's women follow Peacock's in respect to mere formal accomplishments.

---

[26] *Ordeal of Richard Feverel*, Vol. 2, Ch. XII, p. 193.
[27] *Evan Harrington*, Vol. 6, Ch. XVI, p. 203.
[28] *Sandra Belloni*, Vol. 4, Ch. L, p. 223.
[29] *The Adventures of Harry Richmond*, Vol. 9, Chs. XXXVII and XXXVIII, pp. 304–07.
[30] *Beauchamp's Career*, Vol. 12, Ch. XLVI, p. 219.
[31] *The Egoist*, Vol. 13, Ch. XIX, p. 219.
[32] *Diana of the Crossways*, Vol. 16, Ch. XXI, p. 233.
[33] *Ibid.*, Ch. XXVII, pp. 433–35.

The resemblance does not end there, however. The heroines of both Peacock and Meredith are children of the out-of-doors, physically robust and capable. Peacock's women in particular, are active, hardy beings, wanderers of the hills and valleys, students of Nature who find a kind of Wordsworthian inspiration in the survey of wild country. Living in the quiet, green country of the south of England, Meredith's heroines necessarily are less active than some of Peacock's creatures; yet a remarkably large part of their life is spent out-of-doors. Rose Jocelyn rides her horse well; Sandra Belloni seeks refuge in the woods at night as a place native to her spirit; the Princess Ottilia canters on her pony; Cecelia Halkett enjoys the racing of the cutter in the Solent; Clara Middleton is an excellent walker, a lover of country paths, as also is Diana. Aminta is a prodigious swimmer. The most remarkable of Meredith's heroines in physical hardihood, however, and the most like a Peacockian, is his last, Carinthia of *The Amazing Marriage*. Meredith himself describes her as "the naturally straight-growing, untrained, a noble daughter of the woods." Carinthia is dubbed ignorant by her brother, although he recounts her accomplishments in the following paragraph, noteworthy for the number of physical abilities it lists: "You dance well—you ride, you swim, you have a voice—for country songs at all events. You're a bit of a botanist, too. You're good at English and German; you had a French governess for a couple of years. By the way, you understand the use of a walking-stick in self-defense; you can handle a sword on occasion."[34] Carinthia, herself, completes the list by mentioning her competency with pistols. Veritably she is a young Amazon. In physical build, appropriate to her strenuous life, she is heavy; her features too are of a bold, irregular mold, not of a conventional stamp. Her resemblance to Peacock's Miss Susannah Touchango, both in appearance and habit, is striking. Of Miss Touchango, Peacock, putting aside the usual type of heroine, writes, "She was not one of the slender beauties of romance; she was as plump as a partridge."[35] Both heroines too are remarkable for the

---

[34] *The Amazing Marriage*, Vol. 19, Ch. VI, pp. 64–65.
[35] *Crotchet Castle*, Ch. XIV, p. 272.

fondness of lonely rambles and dangerous seats of rest. The discovery of Carinthia by Fleetwood, her future unfortunate husband, atop a precipitous rock, parallels perfectly Susannah's discovery asleep upon a projecting tree limb, by Mr. Chainmail, her future but happy partner.[36] In this case Meredith's imitation of a character and situation is obvious. The fondness of Sandra for wandering, in the woods, is another instance in point, a clear reminiscence from Peacock.

It is not surprising, of course, that Meredith, a great lover of Nature and out-door games, should introduce athletic women in his books; believing in their equality with men, he would naturally allow them the privileges of healthful exercise. But the matter of their presentation really goes deeper than any such personal reason. The athleticism of Meredith's women, as with Peacock's, is apparently a part of a philosophical program for their complete development. As such, it stems from the work of the older man, who, himself a lover of the out-doors life as much as Meredith, evidently made his women strenuous in order definitely to show their superiority over the sheltered, weak women of the conventional type. The physically active woman is to be taken as the natural complement of the mentally free woman: so it is in Peacock, so in Meredith.

As the final quality to be sought and fostered in woman, both Peacock and Meredith agree on an elusive entity called "soul". This soul, evidently, is not the theological soul, but rather a potentiality often smothered out or neglected, a rare spirit born of the maturity and harmonious functioning together of all the faculties, physical and intellectual. It is this fine spiritual flowering that makes of the woman more than a desired physical being, or even a mental companion. Of this quality Meredith wrote, "I am so miserably constituted now that I cannot love a woman if I do not feel her soul, and that there is a force within to wrestle with the facts of life."[37] It was the brutal disregard of this faculty that had made Chloe in *The Tale of Chloe*, remark, "Mr. Beam-

---

[36] *Cf. The Amazing Marriage*, Vol. 19, Ch. XI, pp. 120–22; *Crotchet Castle*, Ch. XIV, pp. 270–72.
[37] *Letters*, Vol. 28, I, p. 54.

ish, we are women, but we have souls."[38] In Peacock this elusive quality, or rather possibility, is not overlooked. There, as in Meredith, all woman's training is regarded simply as a preparation for her to be her best, her finest. In *Melincourt* the thought is well expressed by the idealistic Forrester, who says,[39] "I seek no more than I know to have existed . . . I would have a woman that can love and feel poetry, not only in its harmony and decorations, but in the deep sources of love and liberty . . . she should be musical, but she should have music in her soul as well as her fingers . . . they should be modes of the harmony of her mind." It is toward this perfection of woman that both Peacock and Meredith look. It is their common goal, reached over a common road.

---

[38] *Tale of Chloe*, Vol. 21, p. 205.
[39] *Melincourt*, Ch. XI, p. 88.

VIII

SOURCES AND TYPES OF CHARACTER: FRIENDS, NOTORIETIES, ECCENTRICS

The character of Dr. Middleton in *The Egoist* has been often cited as Meredith's portrait of Peacock.[1] However, it is more than that, for in addition to being something of a life-study, it is also a notable instance of Meredith's reproduction of the stock character types of Peacock's fiction. If Dr. Middleton is Peacock, he is equally a composite of the learned Drs. Folliott and Opimian of *Crotchet Castle* and *Gryll Grange*, respectively. Accordingly, the figure is interesting and significant as a kind of hybrid character developed, at once, under two modes of character creation; both common to Meredith, although more usually employed by him separately than in conjunction. What is more, both of these methods of portraiture had been employed by Peacock himself earlier, and one of them, surely, had been learned by Meredith directly from Peacock's example.

These principles of character composition can perhaps best be approached by a brief discussion of Peacock's practice in that field. And, there, at the out-set, it must be allowed that one of Peacock's greatest deficiencies is his inability to achieve convincing character, to make his people come alive. His heroines, on whom he lavished a loving care, are ideally splendid young women, developed in mind, body and spirit; shrewd and capable in their dealings after the very likeness of the Meredithian woman; yet somehow they are unreal, voices rather than persons. His hosts also vainly make pretense to a certain rude humanity; although uniformly they are good-natured, generous, interested in ideas though personally unfurnished with them, and joyously convivial. They, obviously, are types, and indeed scarcely more than the formal cause for bringing the Peacockian rout together, and the agent reestablishing peace when the war of argument

---

[1] Ellis, S. M., *George Meredith*, London, 1920, p. 262; Priestley, J. B., *George Meredith*, New York, 1926, p. 83.

threatens to mount too high. For the greater part Peacock's characters are "fantasts," men and women possessed by some kind of monomaniacal interest or fixed belief. These people ride hobbies and ideas furiously; they are cranks of all sorts, idealistic reformers, dabbling scientists, amateur philosophers, the type of folk who in life would be called "lunatic." Each and every one, they are caricatures, strongly conceived in terms of governing "humors." Yet, even these people, although unsuccessfully, Peacock endeavors to make live. They are all genial, socially-minded, good citizens, exemplarily moral. Moreover, they are not so intent upon their foibles that they cannot put them away at the calling of a toast or the demand for a glee. Nevertheless, in spite of the slight life-likeness imparted to them by the attribution of human habits and sentiments, these folk remain essentially automata. They are Peacock's puppets called into being "from the void"[2] for the exposition of absurdity, and nothing more.

It is in the grouping of his "fantasts" that Peacock shows his purpose in creating them. To each he assigns a prejudice, a bias, a program, which that character is to defend and promote against all comers. Intellectually, the fellows are nimble; all are equally expert in jesuitical subtlety, with all sorts of telling evidences and ingenious logical fence at their command. As the line of argument passes from one to the other of them, however, their contradictory points of view are shown to be complementary, for each is a segment of truth made contributory to a rounded whole. Truth is discovered on all sides, although the wranglers themselves are unaware of it; all parties are justified, while none is accredited. It is in such fashion, through the mouths of his "fantasts," that Peacock works out the scheme of his own retired, skeptical, yet benignant philosophy. The characters themselves are really the threads of an argument, the logical partitions of a subject, the pro's and con's of debate. They are scarcely more, their urbane manners notwithstanding.

Merged in the group of Peacock's "fantasts," however, is a smaller company, who, though no more vital than the rest, are

---

[2] Saintsbury, George, Introduction to *Melincourt*, pp. VIII and IX.

different in that they pretend at least to be copied from living notables. These are conceived too with a different purpose from the others: they are burlesque characterizations, usually done in very bad temper, and intended to advertise their originals to the public in an unfavorable light. It is in this way that many of Peacock's great contemporaries come to a place in his pages as grotesque caricatures, scarcely recognizable except for the telltale names of epithet pinned to them. In this respect the Lake School of Poets as a groups suffers most; with the Scotch reviewers faring almost equally ill. It was in *Melincourt* that Peacock pilloried the Lakeists for the first time; starting an attack that, with lessened vehemence, was to drag through *Crotchet Castle* later. Coleridge appears in *Melincourt* as Mr. Mystic, Wordsworth as Mr. Paperstamp, and Southey as Mr. Feathernest. The names are interesting for they identify each figure by reference to his profession: Coleridge as transcendental philosopher, Wordsworth as stamp commissioner, Southey as Poet Laureate, i. e. the holder of a sinecure. It is in *Melincourt*, too, that William Gifford the critic is attacked as Mr. Vamp, and George Canning, the statesman, as Mr. Anyside Anti-jack.[3]

Peacock, however, does not always present caricatures of his contemporaries merely to fall furiously upon them. His purpose is always satiric, it is true; but occasionally it is mixed more with laughter than with malice. The picturing of Byron, as Mr. Cypress, in *Nightmare Abbey*,[4] for example, is not to be taken so much as a personal satire, as a criticism well-directed against the whole cult of melancholy romanticism. Moreover, Peacock is not angry; he is only laughing at folly. Even more interesting is his portrait of Shelley in the same novel, whom, in the character of Scythrop, he makes the hero of the piece. Indeed, what Peacock does, covertly, is to take the unhappy situation of Shelley's domestic life for the story of his novel. Scythrop is Shelley, and the two young women between whom he stands, uncertain, in equipoise of attraction, the blonde and the brunette, are Harriet Shelley and Mary Wollstencraft.[5] The women may be dismissed

---

[3] Priestley, J. B., *Thomas Love Peacock*, New York, 1927, Ch. II, pp. 36–37.
[4] Priestley, J. B., *Thomas Love Peacock*, New York, 1927, Ch. XI, p. 149.
[5] *Ibid.*, Ch. II, pp. 41–42.

as types, providing between them only a balance of attractions; but Scythrop is definitely a study of Shelley and the dilemma of his romantic temperament. Of course, no more than the others is Scythrop a true character; but he is vastly amusing, and one develops a mild sympathy for him in his plight. The sketch, however, is important in another respect: it is the only drawing in Peacock's fiction of a contemporary who was also a personal friend. As Shelley's years' old intimate, his pensioner, his correspondent and business agent in England, Peacock was well-acquainted with all the poet's personal affairs. Accordingly, his putting Shelley in a book might seem to involve something of treachery to the trust of friendship. But evidently Peacock did not regard it so. His treatment of Scythrop is entirely kindly; and it is interesting that Shelley himself was most anxious to read the book,[6] although there is the possibility that he may not have understood that he was the chief actor in it. The situation is interesting as an exact parallel of Meredith's own practice later. One thinks instinctively of Stevenson in far-off Samoa awaiting the publication of *The Amazing Marriage* that he might see what Meredith had made of him.[7]

Accordingly, if we have glanced for a time in the direction of Peacock's sources and methods of characterization it is only because they parallel most interestingly, in several respects, Meredith's own. That Meredith implanted in his work the genus of the Peacockian fantast is unquestioned; his books teem with such people. Moreover, their correspondence is not alone in their developed "humors," the dominance in each of some warping bent, for very often Meredith's eccentrics are definitely copies of Peacock's own people. Discussion of this point, however, on which proof is so amply abundant may well be left for the moment. Rather, because Meredith's chief characters are never of that type, but conceived in a realistic style, in the image often of living persons, it is well to look to them first. But here again one discovers a practice that, if not derivative from Peacock, affords certain suggestive similarities to it.

---

[6] Priestly, J. B., *Thomas Love Peacock*, New York, 1927, Ch. II, pp. 41–42.
[7] Hammerton, J. A., *George Meredith*, Edinburgh, 1911, p. 113.

The practice is Meredith's penchant for putting his friends into his novels in unmistakable likeness. Indeed, his habit in that regard is very similar to Peacock's treatment of Shelley; and may have been passed on to him from that example. Again, it may be supposed that the trick originated very simply in that teasing trait of Meredith's nature on which so many have commented.[8] No matter how much Meredith cared for his friends, it was not inconsistent with his affection to rag and flutter them by the honor and embarrassment of a public presentation. So we may explain the fact that although Meredith gives excellent portraits of his friends, they are almost never without a humorous twist here and there, some indication of the eye of the Comic Spirit upon them. But was it not in the same playful spirit that Peacock conceived his Scythrop? The parallel is close not only in choice of subject but in spirit as well.

Another trait that allies many of Meredith's major characters with those of Peacock is the semi-public status of the originals whom they represent. Of course, Meredith was picturing in his people, most often, his friends, and his treatment of them, accordingly, was playfully gentle; whereas Peacock, on the other hand, usually caricatured notables whom he did not know personally, but whom he disliked on account of their policies or opinions. Again, it must be admitted, that our novelists, in the handling of these public figures differ, in the main, both in the purpose for which they are introduced, and the method of presenting them. Peacock shows them with the view of philosophical or political satire, and his method is that of the crudest caricature with tag names to point the identifications. Meredith, on the other hand, utilizes his public figures for the artistic purpose of solid character study, and his method is realistic. In spite, however, of these marked differences in intention and method, the idea of a linking here between Meredith and Peacock does persist through their common discovery of characters among public persons, and their showing of them in such a way that they are plainly identifiable. Further, on occasion, either novelist vio-

---

[8] Clodd, Edward, *George Meredith, Some Recollections, Fortnightly Review*, July, 1909, p. 29. Butcher, Lady Alice, *Memories of George Meredith*, New York, 1919, Ch. I, pp. 10–11.

lates his usual practice, so that temporarily, at least, much of their contradiction is lost. We have seen, for example, how Peacock, in his most dramatic novel, *Headlong Hall*, by his utilization of Shelley's story, suggests most pointedly Meredith's later method of putting his acquaintances in fiction. But, Meredith himself did not confine his attention to the company of his friends; rather he took his interesting characters wherever they appeared in society. Accordingly, we find him writing of notorieties, to him personally unknown, but promising as subjects because of the dramatic values involved in their lives. His undoubted employment of Mrs. Norton as the model for Diana,[9] and his taking of Ferdinand Lassalle and Helene Von Dönniges,[10] together with their whole love tragedy, for the materials of *The Tragic Comedians* are the great examples of his exploitation of public figures. Now what Meredith did in these instances merely duplicates Peacock's manipulation of Shelley's story. In both instances, the novel is nothing more than a version, slightly disguised, of a current scandal. That Peacock knew personally the subject of his tale while Meredith did not know his, is merely incidental. Meredith's two novels and Peacock's one are basically the same kind of work in their sources. Whether Meredith was led into a kind of superior journalistic fiction by the example of Peacock is unprovable; but the parallel raises the question.

Of all Meredith's characters drawn from life it is not necessary to speak here; they have been identified and listed elsewhere.[11] Of that group of characters which represent well-known persons, however, it may be well to say a few words. These people, such as Tracey Runningbrook in *Sandra Belloni*, who is Swinburne; or Blackburn Tuckham of *Beauchamp's Carur*, who is Sir William Hardman; or Vernon Whitford of *The Egoist*, who is Leslie Stephen; or Gower Woodseer, of *The Amazing Marriage*, who is R. L. Stevenson, are interesting because of Meredith's evident wish that they should be identified. The sketches are as far as possible exact portraiture. The picture of Swinburne, for example, is a frank likeness of the man. The red head and blue eyes

---

[9] *Letters*, Vol. 29, II, p. 355.
[10] *Letters*, Vol. 28, I, p. 311.
[11] Ellis, S. M., *George Meredith*, London, 1920, probably gives the most thorough accounting under the several titles of the novels.

of the poet emerge; his sudden enthusiasms and child-like naïveté are shown; and finally, lest the sketch remain unrecognized, it is labelled by the crypto-grammic name of Runningbrook. In like manner, Gower Woodseer gives us the picture of Stevenson, not the sleek, velvet-coated Stevenson later made familiar to the world, but Stevenson, the vagabonding traveller, a rather tatterdemallion fellow, the tramp-like member of the famous Walking Club. And in memory of his Scotch origin, he is given appropriately a Celtic name—not Scotch, but Cymric, Gower Woodseer. The exactness of the physical portraiture in these sketches can be easily ascertained. He, for example, who will compare a picture of Sir William Hardman with the description of Blackburn Tuchkam in *Beauchamp's Career* will be struck by the fidelity of Meredith's portraiture of still another.

The truth is that Meredith sketched these people most carefully, and tagged them too, in order that they might be recognized. The pleasure that he derived from seeing them in his pages, and that his friends would feel also at the spectacle of themselves, played no doubt a large part in dictating their creation. Yet beyond his personal circle, Meredith also must have thought something of a public, a rather select one of course, who might relish novels with characters slightly disguised. This playing with identities is a prominent feature of Meredith's writing always; part evidently of the fun of the game for him. And this same mischievous disposition, one guesses, was part of Peacock's literary mood too. His lay-figures designed to mock celebrities are scarcely more formidable than scare-crows; and scarcely can he have thought of them as more. It was then personal delight, coupled with perception of the piquancy of reference to public characters, that most likely set both Peacock and Meredith writing of living persons, either friends or strangers. The practice in the two men is bound up with very different literary intentions, to be sure; but there is enough in it to point at least an interesting parallel.

On the other hand, the influence of Peacock's purely fantastic characters is certain. Meredith, of course, because he was a genuine investigator of human nature, a student of men and women, rather than a mere speculator, like Peacock, in the realm of abstract philosophy, escaped the limitations of the elder novelist's method. Yet it is surprising how often he employs it; how in the handling both of groups and of individuals he follows the Peacockian formula in the strictest manner. The major characters are not affected by this influence, as need scarcely be said; for they are genuinely Meredith's own, creatures of a human complexity evolved by the patient searcher of nature. But the lesser folk are created as types by the easier, simpler method of Peacock which Meredith chooses consciously to use as better fitting his purpose with them. Where, for example, a group of persons are presented at the dinner table or in a social assembly, the characters may be more quickly and deftly presented by means of caricature than by any other. Moreover, figures presented merely for the moment need to be sharply accentuated if they are to be known at all. Again, the single fantastic figure is most useful as a foil to a greater character, who shows to better advantage because of the nonentity beside him. In this way, Harry Richmond is set off against the humble, inoffensive Prince Hermann, who is an ichthyologist; Beauchamp is provided with the empty-headed Lord Palmet for satellite; and Fleetwood is set beside Lord Feltre, a devotee of religion. Again the fantastic figure is one of general enlivement, providing a note of comic relief to the story; as, for example, do Mr. Pericles, the impresario, and Sir Twickenham Pryme, the Parliamentary statistician, in *Sandra Belloni*.

Still further, to Meredith, always intent on introducing intellectual comedy in his work, the Peacockian "fantast" was indeed too serviceable a device to be discarded. Accordingly, we find the type of Peacockian eccentric retained by Meredith through the whole period of his writing, and, what is more, on occasion, the entire Peacockian gallery reproduced, not only in types of character, but in their grouping and the very manner of their introduction to the reader. As has been pointed out before, in Peacock's larger scenes the "fantasts" are always grouped in order that their contradictions may be brought out in fullest opposition. Then, if the characters have not been met before, they are introduced by having them described, each in turn, in witty epitome, by an observer. In *Crotchet Castle* it is Miss

Crotchet who performs this office for the recently arrived Captain Fitz-chrome, and, incidentally, for the reader.[12] A complete survey of the dinner-company is made by this discerning young woman for the benefit of her bewildered admirer; each guest is pointed out and neatly ticketed. It is this identical trick that Meredith employs in *Evan Harrington*, when, in a letter, the Countess de Saldar describes for her sister the table at Beckley Court. It is the roll-call method of Peacock complete. "First, Mr. Parsley, the curate of Beckley. He eats everything at table and agrees with everything [the very picture of one of Peacock's meaner parsons] . . . Mr. Drummond Forth. A great favorite of Lady Jocelyn's; an old friend . . . Hamilton Jocelyn—all politics. The stiff Englishman. Not a shade of manners. Seymour Jocelyn, Colonel of Hussars. He did nothing but sigh for cold weather and hunting . . . Then there is my Melville, the dear diplomat."[13] Undoubtedly Meredith had the scene in *Crotchet Castle* definitely in mind when he penned the Countess' recital. Nor is this an isolated instance of that sort of scene. Passing down the list of novels to *One of Our Conquerors*, a book remarkable for the recrudescence of Peacockian features of all kinds, we have, in the scene of the great assembly at Lakelands, another reworking of the old formula. There it is Dartrey Fenellan who identifies for Mrs. Blathenoy the notables that swarm in the music-hall; the financier from the City, the master of the bacon market, the army captain, the country squire, the merchant prince; all pass in review.[14] It is the Peacockian meeting of incongruous souls done once again.

It is in *One of Our Conquerors* also that there appears the best formal grouping of "fantasts" in all Meredith. The scene in all its Victor Radnor's house; and around the table are placed Radnor's chosen friends over whom he presides in the indulgent, patronizing fashion of the typical Peacockian host. The company is described as follows: "Priscilla Graves, an eater of meat, was ridiculous in her anti-alcoholic exclusiveness and scorn. Mr.

---

[12] *Crotchet Castle*, Ch. V, pp. 182–186.
[13] *Evan Harrington*, Vol. 6, Ch. XIV, pp. 177–179.
[14] *One of Our Conquerors*, Vol. 17, Ch. XXI, pp. 248–50.

Pempton, a drinker of wine, would laud extravagantly the more transparent purity of vegetarianism. Dr. Peter Yatt jeered at globules. Dr. John Cormyn mourned over human creatures treated as cattle by big doses. The Rev. Septimus Barmby satisfactorily smoked. Mr. Peridon traced mortal evil to that act. Dr. Schliesen had his German views, Colney Durance, his ironic, Fenellan his fanciful and free-lance . . . all of them were pointedly opposed, extraordinarily so for so small an assembly: absurdly, it might be thought: but they provoked a kind, warm smile, with the exclamation: 'They are dears'."[15] Here, about the board, are ranged with a calculated nicety those pairs of mutually opposed minds that are the mechanism of Peacockian comedy. An added similarity to the scheme of Peacock is found in the fact, unmentioned in the quoted passage, that the one common interest that these people have is a love of music. Music it is that draws them of evenings to Radnor's house; and music it always is in the Peacockian drawing-room that after clamorous argument unites the company in peace. The parallel is perfect in all parts. Further, the desultory play of these characters with their cross-opinions through the length of the novel, as a kind of comic relief to the tragic theme, is accomplished just as in Peacock. These fantastic folk never develop, never become real in any sense; they continue their little wars to the end, without changing a shade of opinion. The sole difference of Meredith's management of these folk from Peacock's is that he keeps them strictly subordinate to the major characters; in Peacock they are truly important, for they are the show itself.

Beside the little people just mentioned there is, in *One of Our Conquerors*, a second group of figures of secondary importance who taken together with Victor Radnor, the central figure of the story, suggest strikingly through their utterances and Meredith's comment upon them, the famous trio with whose introduction Peacock opens *Headlong Hall*. Mr. Foster, the perfectibilian; Mr. Escot, the deteriorationist; and Mr. Jenkinson, the statu-quo-ite, once met are unforgettable.[16] And of them, Victor Radnor, Simeon Fenellan, and Colney Durance, are definitely analogues. Mere-

---

[15] *One of Our Conquerors*, Vol. 17, Ch. VIII, p. 75.
[16] *Headlong Hall*, Ch. I, pp. 9–13.

dith tells us that "the three with their bright view, and black view, and neutral view of life were a comical trio."[17] They, like Peacock's characters represent the basic human temperaments, sanguine, melancholic, and phlegmatic. It is interesting, too, that only one of the three is realized effectively as a human being; the other two are merely foils to the Conqueror, and Durance, in particular, is little more than one continual tirade on the state of England, a character even less human and infinitely less entertaining than Peacock's Mr. Escot. The warfare, as in Peacock, naturally occurs chiefly between the representatives of the extremes; between Radnor and Durance whom Meredith describes as "champion duellists for the rosy and the saturnine." Again, Meredith calls them "the Optimist and Pessimist of their society;" adding, "They might have headed those tribes in the country." In all these things there echoes the remembrance of *Headlong Hall*. What is the more remarkable about these traces of Peacock is their appearance, so distinct, in one of Meredith's latest books. But, as has already been stated, the influence of Peacock, instead of passing with time, seems in fact to have grown stronger. Certainly, the remembrances in *One of Our Conquerors* are not vague, but startlingly exact.

The Peacockian type of eccentric, however, does not always reappear in Meredith's pages as one of a group; frequently, he appears singly, and isolated eccentrics are to be found in practically every novel. Sometimes their rôle is quite subordinate; sometimes they are given an integral place in the action of the novel. The series begins in *Richard Feverel* and does not close until *The Amazing Marriage*. The most remarkable fact about these characters is, however, that although some of them exhibit more than a trace of the influence of Dickens, and others have original peculiarities given to them by Meredith; still the influence of Peacock appears as a formative element in their make-up; while what is more important, a large group of them merely reproduce characters taken out of Peacock without any change of their basic selves at all. Of the less purely Peacockian char-

---

[17] *One of Our Conquerors*, Vol. 17, Ch. XIX, pp. 212–13.

acters, Tom Cogglesby of *Evan Harrington* is an interesting example. This character reproduces very definitely the likeness of either one of the amazing Cheerybyle brothers of Dicken's *Nicholas Nickleby;* indeed it is as obviously Dickensian as any thing that Meredith created. Yet even in Tom Cogglesby there is a definite touch of Peacock too. In the first place, his institution of a birthday wassail at the Green Dragon draws him close to the company of Peacock's genial hosts. But the resemblance does not rest only on such a generality; in particular his "Toast to the Antediluvians, inspired by his theory that the constitutions of the Post-diluvians have been deranged and their lives shortened by the miasmas of the Deluge,"[18] places him in Peacock's school of deteriorationists, and affiliates him definitely with the eccentric Mr. Firedamp of *Crotchet Castle* who saw in water the principle of death.[19] Another character of Meredith's who, in spite of obvious Dickensian features, shows an equal derivation from Peacock is the ubiquitous Skepsey of *One of Our Conquerors*. The little clerk with his physical demonstrativeness is a Dicken's portrait unmistakable; but his intellectual mania is Peacockian.[20] His gospel of pugilism as a means of training the masses for national defense is exactly the sort of half-mad notion with which Peacock has his characters obsessed; moreover, Meredith in giving Skepsey his idea is merely following out Peacock's old method of discussing public problems that interested him through the imperfect solutions of whimsical characters. Still another of Meredith's characters of mixed development in whom we still catch sight of Peacock's example is Mr. Pericles, the multi-millionaire impresario, of *Sandra Belloni* and *Vittoria*.[21] His love of music suggests Peacock's musical crotcheteers, of whom there are quite a few; and his quest of a golden voice, more particularly, the uncommon zeal of Peacock's fanatic scientists who search indefatigably for all sorts of rare things from the skulls of celebrities to mermaids.

One of the clearest reminiscences of Peacock's characterization

---

[18] *Evan Harrington*, Vol. 6, Ch. XII, pp. 143–44.
[19] *Crotchet Castle*, Ch. II, p. 156.
[20] *One of Our Conquerors*, Vol. 17, Ch. IV, p. 27.
[21] *Sandra Belloni*, Vol. 3, Ch. I, pp. 1–16.

in Meredith's early work is found in the person of Uncle Hippias, "the Dyspepsy," of *Richard Feverel*.[22] His imaginary ailments ally him with the paranoiacs of *Headlong Hall*, and his *Fairy Mythology of Europe* places him among Peacock's eccentric scholars and scientists in a double bond of relationship.[23] In the same manner *Sandra Belloni* in Sir Twickenham Pryme contains one of the most perfect examples of Peacock's method of characterization in all Meredith.[24] Except that Meredith has endowed his character with a new sort of foible, not found in Peacock, the figure might well seem to be taken bodily out of the elder man's work, so perfectly, in method and spirit, does it reproduce the genius of Peacock's eccentrics. Sir Twickenham thinks and speaks wholly in terms of figures: his conversation is of percentages, rates, and proportions; statistics enter inevitably into his every utterance. The idea is original with Meredith, but the effect of the character, developed so exclusively in terms of "humor," is pure Peacock, as genuine as Peacock's own.

The novel *Harry Richmond* opens, surprisingly enough, on a strong note of Peacockian reminiscence. The characters of Squire Beltham and his faithful servant Sewis, in the opening chapter at least, amply suggest as their antecedents, Mr. Humphrey Hippy and his servant, Harry Fell, of *Melincourt*.[25] Not only are both Squire Beltham and Mr. Humphrey Hippy choleric to a marked degree, but both have a hatred for medicine, and a fear of its being forced upon them—a peculiar point of similarity. Squire Beltham's instant suspicion of a visit from the apothecary when he was awakened early in the morning by his servant, quite evidently looks back to Mr. Hippy's dislike of the doctor's visits and the nauseous draughts he brought.[26] Of course, after the first chapter, the parallel breaks down and is lost, for Meredith proceeds to develop his characters away from the model of Peacock; but for the moment, a parallel is distinct. Another character

---

[22] *Cf.* Ellis, S. M., *George Meredith*, London, 1920, p. 99 for the actual portrait work also involved here.
[23] *Ordeal of Richard Feverel*, Vol. 2, Ch. XX, p. 158.
[24] *Sandra Belloni*, Vol. 3, Ch. X, pp. 80-82.
[25] *Cf. Adventures of Harry Richmand*, Vol. 9, Ch. I, pp. 1-4; *Melincourt*, Ch. III, pp. 22-26.
[26] *Cf. Ibid.*, Ch. I, p. 3; Ch. VIII, p. 63.

in the same novel that develops an erstwhile figure of Peacock's is Prince Hermann. The prototype of this pleasant, and well-mannered, although temperamentally weak prince is undoubtedly Lord Curryfin of *Gryll Grange*. Not only are both the prince and the nobleman of the same gentle nature, equally modest in their pursuit of love, but both, as the decisive link of identification between them, ride a common hobby, the study of ichthyology.[27] Curryfin is an enthusiast who lectures on the subject of fish to anyone who will listen, from old fishermen to society ladies; Lord Hermann, equally in earnest, is a collector of fish specimens and projects a musem. Again we have a parallel too close for accident.

In *Beauchamp's Career*, the character of Beauchamp, which is to be taken as the literary representation of Augustus Maxse, Meredith's dearest friend whose reforming principles made him a man of interest, seems not without its affiliation also to Peacock's character of Falconer, the idealistic reformer of *Melincourt*. In inflexibility of belief, and imperviousness to the teaching of experience, the two figures are exactly alike. The thought of a literary parallel here, however, is heightened if attention is given to the figures which are given respectively to Falconer and Beauchamp as foils. The likeness of Lord Palmet, Beauchamp's friend, to Sir Telegraph Paxarett, Falconer's companion, is striking. The type in both instances is of a young nobleman, rich and ignorant, given over to frivolities, but of good temper, and amenable, temporarily, to social instruction from his high-minded friend. In short, both Palmet and Sir Telegraph present the same amusing and pitiable picture of a life wasted through faulty education and unthinking self-indulgence. The analogue is quite perfect; and sufficient to convince one that Meredith, although he might be picturing his friend in Beauchamp, also had his eye definitely set on Peacock's performance in *Melincourt*.

This chapter on Meredith's characters and the ways in which they reflect Peacock's work must necessarily stand incomplete,

---

[27] Cf. *Adventures of Harry Richmond*, Vol. 10; Ch. XXXIV, p. 29; *Gryll Grange*, Ch. XIII, p. 85.

not only because the characters are too numerous for detailed analysis, but because such an analysis is unnecessary here owing to the appearance of the characters in other chapters where their affiliation with Peacock's thought is indicated in its own particular sphere. Rather is the purpose of the chapter a more general one: an attempt merely to point out by illustration how Meredith took the type of the Peacockian "fantast" and utilized it for the purpose of his own art. That he did so is almost beyond controversy, since his people so often, although they bear a greater similitude to living beings than Peacock's, are only Peacock's eccentrics revived, both in thought and habit. And beyond this certain linking, there rises another resemblance, somewhat vague and tenuous but not without suggestion, in the common use by the two novelists of living notorieties and current gossip in their books. That Meredith was the creator of men and women, while Peacock, at his best, but the etcher of silhouettes is beside the question: that there was a common denominator in the sources of their characterization and in their type of people is the real matter. And of this the evidences have been presented.

IX

The Discovery of the Celt

Among the championships and enthusiasms to which Meredith freely gave himself not the least is his often-expressed admiration for the Celt and all things Celtic. Through his novels, from *Evan Harrington* on to *Celt and Saxon*, this interest finds constant expression. His letters, moreover, confirm the interest and show how personal and intense it really was. In them Meredith proudly proclaims himself a Celt, glorying in his heritage of Celtic blood. "I draw my blood mainly from the Cymric and can understand enthusiasm," he writes in one place[1] Such a statement is significant as showing the force of Meredith's sentiments on this subject and indicating the racial pride that fostered them. In one sense, of course, there is nothing very strange about this racial identification of Meredith's, for ultimately he derived on both sides of the house from Celtic stock; and it is not unusual for a man to take pride in his ancestry and to have a sentimental attachment for the land of his fathers, a land which perhaps he has never visited but which is the more glamorous on that very account. Particularly in a romantic temperament like Meredith's such a pride is quite easily explicable. Moreover, racial traits are strangely persistent, and Meredith quite likely perceived in himself, truly enough, the out-cropping of those psychical traits that throughout the centuries have distinguished the Celts from their less volatile Saxon neighbors. The imagination of the Celt, his poetical insight, his love of truth and his love of freedom, together with his ardent mystical nature: all these characteristics were Meredith's own in generous measure; and, recognizing them in himself, he rightly regarded them as the endowment of racial genius, the persistent reassertion in him, the individual, of the age-old spirit of his people. It was indeed discovery born of true insight; and the eagerness with which he embraced it is, in itself, a testimony of his Celtic warmth of feeling.

---

[1] *Letters*, Vol. 29, II, p. 419.

However, although one can easily see the Celt in Meredith, the man, and in his work as an artist, and sympathetically understand why he was proud of the line that had so richly dowered him in the things of the spirit; it is a matter for consideration when he became racially conscious. In the first place, it is not true biologically, however it may be temperamentally, that Meredith was predominantly Celtic. It must be remembered that the Merediths were three generations removed from Wales; his mother's people, two generations from Ireland.[2] By intermarriage in either branch the tide of Saxon blood must have encroached upon the Celtic so that the latter could scarcely be the dominant strain in Meredith. Accordingly his statement about his Celtic blood gives but a half-truth that chooses to blink the facts. Under the power of that same imaginative force that enabled him so well to dramatize various aspects of his life, to make him, staunch Britisher, declare himself an internationalist;[3] and, even to the end, amid honours, to complain of himself as an unappreciated man; he chose too sometimes to forget the Saxon element in his make-up.

Now this romancing about the Celt, like the other attitudes that Meredith built into his life, one suspects dates not from childhood but from the period of his young manhood. Indeed, it would seem that Meredith's knowledge of and appreciation of the Celt must first have come through a connection outside his family; and that not until that tie was made could he have thought of himself as, or declared himself, a Celt. Consideration of a point so personal cannot well be other than inferential, but evidences are not utterly lacking to guide one toward such a conclusion. To begin with, there is nothing to show that the Merediths thought of themselves as anything other than English. Their name, of course, still proclaimed their origin; but such is the habit of names to do, long after all sense of foreignness has been lost by those that bear them. Moreover, from the picture that Meredith gives us of Old Mel, his grandfather, and from what may be gathered from other sources, there is little to indicate the con-

---

[2] Ellis, S. M., *George Meredith*, London, 1920, pp. 18–19; pp. 33–34.
[3] *Letters*, Vol. 28, I, p. 122.

tinuance of any marked Celtic traits among the Merediths, much less any sense among them of racial separateness from their neighbors. And if Old Mel talked largely of princely ancestors in dim Welsh history (his only reference to the subject) it was with the object of stressing the nobility of that descent, not its Welshness.[4] The real distinction of Old Mel was his ability to pass as a gentleman—a gentleman among Saxon gentlemen in the distinctively Old English county of Hampshire. Again it is significant that the Merediths were Church of England people; if they had brought from Wales the dissenting faith of which most Welshmen are so tenacious, they had abandoned it long since. Apparently, on all grounds, they were part and parcel of the community in which they were comfortably settled.

Likewise, of the Irish stock on the mother's side, one hears nothing to make one regard it as a possible influence in the fertilizing of Meredith's Celtic sympathies; as, indeed, it could scarcely have been, owing to his mother's death in his early years. Moreover, it is quite apparent that Meredith's championship of the Irish in his later books is to be taken only as the logical extension of his Cymric sympathies to the rest of the Celtic family at large. His Celtic enthusiasm was always primarily Cymric, and it is evidently to the paternal line that he appeals first when he claims place as a Celt. But if the sense of racial identity could scarcely have come from his home, less possibly could it have come out of his schooling. His experience of schools either in England or at Neuwied, in Germany, can have given him nothing of the kind; for, apart from their remoteness from all things Celtic, it is the nature of public schools to destroy rather than to build up any sense of clanship outside themselves. Indeed, in the whole length of Meredith's career there is discoverable only one contact whereby a Celtic influence of a broad cultural sort could have reached him; namely, his association with Thomas Love Peacock. But this one source is all sufficient to explain Meredith's kindling enthusiasm for the Celt. When he adopted himself into heart-felt kinship with the Welsh, he was only doing, with the more ample justification of ancestry, what

---

[4] *Evan Harrington*, Vol. 6, Ch. II, p. 11.

Peacock had almost done before him. The elder novelist, with his amateur's knowledge of Wales, the country, her people, and her literature, was well prepared to be Meredith's mentor; that he was literally the guide to Meredith's discovery of his racial kin is scarcely to be doubted.

Thomas Love Peacock was not Welsh, himself, but of Scotch descent. His connections with Wales, however, had been of such sort as to make him familiar with many phases of that nation's life and tradition, and to instill in him a deep admiration of things Welsh. As a young man he had tramped the mountains of North Wales, discovering for himself those beauties of wild and rugged scenery that were later to appear in the characteristic descriptions of his novels. Among those mountains, too, he had found his wife, Jane Gryffydh to whom, after an interval of eight years, he had proposed by post.[5] Something of the Cymric tongue he must have gained upon his excursions into Wales, as may be inferred not only from passages in his novels where the casual learning of the tongue by strangers is mentioned,[6] but by his genuine interest in the literature of Wales which he ransacked for the materials of The *Misfortunes* of *Elphin;* [7] and which, as a whole, had not as yet been made available in English translation.[8]

In all, Wales is the scene of four of Peacock's novels. *Headlong Hall* (1816), his first, pictures the Vale of Llanberris, in South Wales, the same country that is the scene of *The Misfortunes of Elphin* (1829). The scene of the fragmentary *Caledore* (1816), is also laid for the greater part in Wales. Likewise, *Crotchet Castle* (1831) has part of its action laid in North Wales whither the inhabitants of the Castle go on excursion. Elsewhere, as in *Melincourt*, although the scene has been shifted to Cumberland, one feels that Peacock is still describing his favorite Welsh country. Of all Peacock's Welsh books, however, *The Misfortunes of*

---

[5] Priestley, J. B., *Thomas Love Peacock*, New York, 1927, pp. 177–178.
[6] *Crotchet Castle*, Ch. I, p. 147.
[7] Priestley, J. B., *Thomas Love Peacock*, New York, 1927, pp. 177–178; Strachey, Sir Edward: *Recollections of Thomas Love Peacock* in *Calidore and Miscellanea*, London, 1891, p. 19.
[8] Maclean, Magnus, *The Literature of the Celts*, London, 1906, pp. 216–17, or Skene, W. F., *The Four Ancient Books of Wales*, Edinburgh, 1868, Vol. I, pp. 4–8.

Elphin is undoubtedly the most interesting because not only the scene but the subject too is Welsh. Although one cannot be sure exactly what source or sources Peacock employed for the legendary material of his novel, which was taken from all four of the *Four Ancient Books of Wales*, it must have been either the various translations that had appeared scatteredly during the second half of the 18th Century of individual Welsh poems; or, in the original tongue, the *Myvyrian Archaeology* that appeared between 1801 and 1807. The fact that *The Misfortunes of Elphin* is a *mélange* of themes and characters taken at random from all four of the bardic books, and recombined and adapted with the greatest freedom, seems to point to the use of some such convenient collection as the *Myvyrian Archaeology*, or, otherwise, the use of the combined translations that various hands up that time, had made available. How great a mastery Peacock had of the Welsh language, a speech notoriously difficult for the foreigner, to help him in the reading of it, it is of course, impossible to say. One suspects, however, that a proficient in languages like Peacock, a man always self taught, could make way for himself there as in the more familiar classical tongues. Moreover, his wife was Welsh, and could be of help.

The similarity of the references, in Peacock and Meredith, to Welsh legend make it evident that they both derived their knowledge in that field from the same source or sources, for they speak of the same persons and the same events, and neither more nor less than the full regular number. When in *The Amazing Marriage*, speaking of the Welsh, Meredith writes: "They march still with Cadwallader, sing with Aneurin, Taliesin, old Llywarch,"[9] the passage is arresting because it packs into a single notice all the company of those heroes to whom Peacock had given attention. Especially is the juxtaposition of the names of Aneurin, Taliesin, and old Llywarch striking, because in *The Misfortunes of Elphin* these worthies are thrown together and treated as rival poets and singers.[10] Evidently, Meredith too thinks of them as constituting a group; at least, he does not

---

[9] *The Amazing Marriage*, Vol. 19, Ch. XXVIII, p. 296.
[10] *The Misfortunes of Elphin*, Ch. XV, pp. 117–125.

bother to differentiate them: for him, collectively, as for Peacock, they are "The Bards of Old Britain."

Again, Meredith draws close to his and Peacock's common literary source when he makes reference to the spirit and form of Welsh verse. For the *awen* (inspiration) of the bard he had respect; and of the various measures and tropes, he seems to have had a fair technical knowledge. The Triad, the usual form for Welsh gnomic utterance, with its three inter-related propositions, Meredith regarded highly as a subtle form of composition worthy of study. At least such an opinion is to be inferred from a speech he gives to Gower Woodseer in *The Amazing Marriage*, and all his other references to the Triad only confirm it:[11] "But those Triads. They're in our blood. They spring to tie knots in my head. They press to condense my thoughts to a tight ball. They were good for primitive times." The composing of a Triad, perhaps, represented an intellectual task not unlike that which Meredith set for himself in his own writing in its succinct statement of wisdom. Such may have been the secret of his fondness for the Triads. Accordingly it is amusing to contrast this attitude of reverent interest with the levity of Peacock who mentions the Triads no less often. For Peacock the Triads were merely matter for humorous citation. He writes of "The Three Chaste Kisses of the Island of Britain," or "The Three Fatal Slaps of the Island of Britain" in the spirit of burlesque.[12] For him the Triads were neither deep sayings nor well-contrived. But, in any case, no matter what the quality of their appreciation, it is sure that both he and Meredith are regarding the same originals, consulting probably the same books.

This evident use of a common source of information immediately suggests the question whether Meredith knew Welsh at all. That Peacock knew the tongue, in a fumbling way at least, seems fairly clear; his travels, his marriage, his penchant for linguistic studies privately pursued make it likely. But Meredith enjoyed no like opportunities; yet from his mention of the technical terms of Welsh verse he would seem to know the poetry in its

---

[11] *The Amazing Marriage*, Vol. 19, Ch. XVIII, p. 191.
[12] *The Misfortunes of Elphin*, Ch. VIII, p. 62.

original forms. Accordingly, two possible assumptions present themselves: either Meredith under the inspiration of Peacock's leadership undertook the study of the Welsh tongue, which, although it is notoriously difficult, his new-born racial pride would make him eager to know; or, what seems far more likely, he learned of the Welsh literature solely from what Peacock gave him in his novels and in his conversation; and from the various translations which Peacock's library most probably contained, the fruit of his own amateur interest. In any case, whichever method was the actual one, the coincidence of the references to Welsh literature in Peacock and Meredith is explained, and a new and interesting link forged in the history of their relationship.

Apart from their similarity in historical literary reference, Meredith's reproduction of scenes and incidents from Peacock's Welsh novels, too, is striking. Meredith's folk, like Peacock's, often find it pleasant or expedient to vacation in Wales. Colonel de Craye of *The Egoist*,[13] for instance, tells of a friend "who rowed his bride . . . up the Thames to the Siwan, on into North Wales." It is noteworthy that this trip follows the exact route of the boat-party in *Crotchet Castle*.[14] Cecelia Halkett in *Beauchamp's Career* is taken into Wales in order that she may forget her lover[15]; an action anticipated by Miss Susannah Touchandgo of *Crochet Castle* who made the journey for the same purpose.[16] In *Sandra Belloni*, the heroine is taken into Wales to a Christmas ball of the identical sort given by the jovial master of Headlong Hall in the novel of that name.[17] The episode of the coach halted on the wintry road quite manifestly harks back to the coaching difficulties of Squire Headlong's guests. The brief description of the ball itself is pure Peacock. Again Carinthia Fleetwood in *The Amazing Marriage* is banished by her husband to his castle in Wales where, like a true chatelaine, she wins the love of all the neighborhood. The lonely and unprotected condition of Carinthia suggests the plight of Anthelia the heroine of

[13] *The Egoist*, Vol. 13, Ch. XXII, pp. 254–55.
[14] *Crotchet Castle*, Ch. IX, p. 147.
[15] *Beauchamp's Career*, Vol. 12, Ch. XXXVII, p. 418.
[16] *Crotchet Castle*, Ch. I, p. 147.
[17] *Cf. Sandra Belloni*, Vol. 4, pp. 187–88; *Crotchet Castle*, Ch. XIII, pp. 100–109.

Melincourt, but, more than that, the mock description of an Eisteddfod, in which rumor pictures Carinthia as queen, parallels perfectly the burlesque treatment of the bardic festival in *The Misfortunes of Elphin*.[18] The incident, too, in *Sandra Belloni* when Sandra laments over her broken harp, declaring that it can never be replaced by another, is interesting as re-echoing another episode of *The Misfortunes of Elphin;* namely, the lament of the old bard at having to cast away his harp, which he would almost rather die with than lose.[19] Another reference to this same episode comes again in *Celt and Saxon* where the sentiment of Welsh women for the ancestral harp is mentioned.[20] Such are some of the unmistakable reproductions of Peacock's Welsh material in Meredith's novels.

It is characteristic, however, of Meredith that having discovered his racial inheritance through the agency of Peacock, and become a Celt, he should be a more strenuous admirer of the Cymry than his teacher. Peacock truly admired Welsh scenery and put a sentimental value on Welsh women, and enjoyed Welsh literature as a kind of rude curiosity; but true to his unenthusiastic temperament he refused to regard either people or culture with any idealization. In fact, one feels that Peacock found the Welsh rather ludicrous. Their pride of ancestry he makes the subject of ridicule in *Headlong Hall*, where he traces down the mythical line of the Ap Headlongs from the time of the Flood.[21] In their poetry, too, he finds more of amusement than of intrinsic worth, as is indicated when he speaks of the poems of Taliesin, "which have neither head nor tail, and which having no sense in any other point of view, must necessarily, as a learned mythologist has demonstrated, be assigned to the class of theology in which an occult sense can be found or made for them, according

---

[18] *Cf. The Amazing Marriage*, Vol. 19, Ch. XXXIV, p. 351; *The Misfortunes of Elphin*, Ch. XV, pp. 117–125.
[19] *Cf. Sandra Belloni*, Vol. 3, Ch. XII, pp. 101–102; *The Misfortunes of Elphin*, Ch. III, p. 24.
[20] *Celt and Saxon*, Vol. 20, Ch. VI, p. 40.
[21] *Headlong Hall*, Ch. I, pp. 5–6.

to the views of the expounder."[22] The niceties of the Triads, with their gnomic wisdom, apparently had little appeal to him. He imitates the form of the Triad but only to give a humorous twist to his own style, and uses them for quotation only in a humorous way. The mysteries of the Druidic religion he dismisses as so much "allegorical mummery."[23] And yet, in spite of slights of this sort, it is evident that Peacock had a genuine liking for the Welsh. Only he refused to see them as different from the rest of the human species.

It is here that Meredith turns away from Peacock. To Meredith the Welsh are definitely a people set apart not only by geography, history, and culture, but by a spiritual difference. At times, it is true, he does seem to have much of Peacock's laughing attitude toward the Welsh, especially in regard to their pride of race. For example we are told in *Evan Harrington* that Old Mel "in his cups, talked largely and wisely of a great Welsh family, issuing from a line of princes."[24] It is to this glorious claim that, late in the book, the Countess de Saldar refers when she asks, "Were we Tudors, according to Papa? or only Powys chieftains?"[25] In the same mocking vein, in *Harry Richmond*, Meredith passes comment on Richmond Roy's Welsh heiress: "She was well-born, of course—she was Welsh."[26] Likewise, even so late as *The Amazing Marriage* and *Celt and Saxon* he makes fun of Welsh customs and prejudices. But to laugh at the Welsh is with Meredith the exceptional case, not the rule. Rather he is the glorifier of things Welsh. He admires them for their unique qualities of poetic imagination, of stalwart independence, and of loyalty. Unlike Peacock, Meredith is convinced of the positive merits of the Welsh people and of the excellence of their literature. What with Peacock had been merely interesting because of its difference, takes on for Meredith a definite superiority. In keep-

---

[22] *The Misfortunes of Elphin*, Ch. VI, p. 45. Peacock's reference here to "a learned mythologist" may indicate the Rev. Edward Davies, author of *The Mythology of the British Bards*, 1809, who sponsored the theory of a mystical interpretation for the poems. For the significance of Davies' work see Skene's Introduction to *The Four Ancient Books of Wales*, pp. 7–8.
[23] *Ibid.*, p. 45.
[24] *Evan Harrington*, Vol. 6, Ch. II, p. 11.
[25] *Ibid.*, Ch. XLVI, pp. 562–63.
[26] *Harry Richmond*, Vol. 9, Ch. XX, p. 232.

ing with this prideful belief, Welsh virtues are lauded all through Meredith. He presents Welsh character, discusses Welsh nature, which he says is different from human nature, sends his people into Wales on various occasion, for recuperation or pleasure, and refers to the glories of Welsh literature and Welsh history again and again.

Ireland and the Irish, because they too are of the Celtic fold, also secure Meredith's attention, especially when in later years he became increasingly politically minded. But Ireland was to Meredith an as yet unassimilated Wales. Accordingly it is noteworthy that in Meredith's last, unfinished novel, bearing the significant title *Celt and Saxon*, both the Welsh and Irish are introduced together. Their differences, as in religion, are set off; but, more important, their likenesses are indicated, their common bond of quick nature against the heavy, unintelligent Saxon. Indeed, in this novel Meredith seeks to show that even Wales is only partly digested; that after centuries of contact England and Wales are very imperfectly fused. Yet such fusion is patently his hope for the future of the kingdom; for him the salvation of the British state lies in the enrichment that only the Celt can bring.[27] On this point it is significant that Meredith's Celtic picture is incomplete in that he never introduces a Scots character nor makes reference to the Northern kingdom; evidently he regarded Scotland as thoroughly Saxonized. Such is the natural inference, for Meredith celebrates the Celt wherever he is found. In *One of Our Conquerors*, for example, he speaks of the Breton Celts of France, holding them accountable, apparently, for the phenomenon of French wit.[28] Indeed, Meredith is the champion of the Celt in general; he believes in the breed and its intrinsic qualities, not only for itself, but as a leaven which may leaven the Saxon lump, and bring new vitality and imagination to the whole British race.

The surprising fact about Meredith's Celtic interest, however, apart from its generous enthusiasm, is the degree in which it follows and, apparently, is limited by the performance of Peacock.

---

[27] *Celt and Saxon*, Vol. 20, Ch. XVI, pp. 165–85.
[28] *One of Our Conquerors*, Vol. 17, Ch. XI, p. 111.

It must be remembered that Meredith did not know Wales at first hand. There is record of but one short trip to South Wales that he made late in his life; nothing more.[29] Consequently he was practically compelled in writing of Wales and or Ireland to rely on the second-hand information of books or the observations of such characters as society threw in his way. Accordingly, Meredith often gives his leading characters a Celtic origin without, apart from the intended compliment of their Welsh or Irish birth, realizing in them any special racial traits. Merthyr Powys, the quiet and unbelievably restrained hero of *Sandra Belloni* and *Vittoria*, is made a Welshman. But in this instance it seems that Meredith is scarcely using more than the label of his most favored nation to cover his hero. In essence, Merthyr is of the same faithful nature as Redworth in *Diana*, who is a "dull and creeping Saxon." Likewise, Diana of the Crossways is represented as deriving her wit from an Irish father; but, except for a certain vivacity, she might well be English. So too with Victor Radnor and Lord Fleetwood, both of whom we are told were of old Welsh stock: there is nothing distinctively Celtic about them; they are merely furnished with nationality by their creator's whim. So it is that the attribution of Celtic blood to chief characters is largely interesting as showing how persistently the thought of the Celt came to Meredith's mind. His Celtic characters are no more wise or successful than their Saxon counterparts in the other novels; he favors them in no such special way. But although they are given no cheap victories, their racial strain is trumpeted to such good effect that one becomes aware of the existence of the Celtic element in British life, and of the tremendous value that Meredith places on it as the quickener of the national wit and energy. Meredith, the Celt, is veritably championing his race, calling attention to the Celtic remnant, claiming a place, and a high one, for them. He who has read Meredith can scarcely remain unimpressed by the fact of their existence; most likely he will feel a lively sense of their import-

---

[29] Ellis, S. M., *George Meredith*, London, 1921, p. 284.

ance. And undoubtedly this is the result that Meredith sought to achieve. Accordingly, there is something mildly ironical in the knowledge that he, himself, was a convert to the cause he sponsored, a discoverer of his people, led back to them by the help of a renegade Scotsman with an amateur's flare for Welsh antiquities. But such it can scarcely be doubted was actually one of Peacock's most useful offices to Meredith.

X

A Point of Style

In the prose style of Meredith, so often arraigned for its awkward difficulty, as in so many other particulars, it is possible to trace a distinct influence of Peacock. This is not to say that Meredith owed his manner of expression, or that complete philosophy of rhetoric which governed it, to the elder man. For the major part, Meredith's style stands free; it is truly his own creation, a unique medium, almost a new language, which he invented for the setting forth of his ideas. Of the theory that underlay this puzzling style he has written in many places, both in his letters and in his novels. Of the resources of our English tongue he was a keen analyst; and on all its treasures he put a proper value. In the beginning of the *Up to Midnight* dialogues, he sums up appreciatively the sources of the native idiom. "And concerning our power of giving," he writes, "are we not England, Scotland, Ireland, with the principality of Wales, and a seasoning from America like a whiff of Atlantic brine? English is solid, Scottish is shrewd, Irish a jet; and there you have earth, well, and water; a sober source, a receptacle for infiltration, and a lively abundance. Cambrian seized by his *Awen* is a boiling geyser. And all of them combined, with their interfusions and their varieties, not forgetting the pungent flavor of *Das Americanismus* coming over them occasionally . . . ; all then, I repeat, so hearty and downright, so sly, so voluble, so fiery, are a guarantee of spirit."[1]

In spite, however, of this tribute to the quality of the tongue, Meredith seems to have felt it inadequate for the expression of the emotional subtleties that were the stuff of his fiction. In one of his letters, addressed to his son, Arthur, he complains of "the difficulty in dealing with a language part of which is dead matter."[2] It is in accordance with this belief that the language in its more

---

[1] *Up to Midnight*, Boston, 1913, p. 2.
[2] *Letters*, Vol. 28, I, p. 321.

ordinary usage is comparatively ineffective as an agent of spirited expression, that Meredith is compelled to discover new modes of utterance. And it is here that he is confronted with his practical dilemma, for he sees there are only two ways by which fresh terms can be secured; either the language must borrow from foreign sources, or elevate into accepted use the language of the streets and fields. Between these two possibilities Meredith does not hesitate; to one of his classical training and aristocratic taste, the borrowing or coining of words from foreign sources seemed infinitely preferable to the legitimization of slang. It is in a dialogue in *One of Our Conquerors* that he presents the horns of the problem, " 'But a pirate-tongue, cut off from its roots, must continue to practice piracy, surely, or else take reinforcements in slang, otherwise it is inexpressive of new ideas.'

" 'Possibly the new ideas are best expressed in slang.'

" 'If insular. They will consequently be incommunicable to foreigners. You would then have us trading with tokens instead of precious currency? Yet I cannot perceive the advantage of letting our ideas be clothed so racy of the obscener soil; considering the pretensions of the English language to become universal. If we refuse additions from above, they force themselves on us from below.' "[3]

It was in accordance with this decision to eschew the "Thameswater English of commerce and drainage," that Meredith turned to the "upper wells," the classical fountains from which, when the Anglo-Saxon sources failed, he drew the words he needed. His literary ideal first of all, however, seems to have been to exploit all the resources of the language; to achieve a balanced style, giving full play both to the Germanic and Latin elements, combining and harmonizing them in the interest of the fullest, richest expression. Accordingly, Meredith came a bold innovator, a daring empiricist in style, wrestling with words to force from them startling images. This he does by impressing the old words into new uses, giving them new applications; and by fantastical

---

[3] *One of Our Conquerors*, Vol. 17, Ch. XXI, p. 246.

metaphor. Let an example suffice to illustrate the method: the description of a stormy London sky in *One of Our Conquerors*. We are told,[4] "A gusty bosom of sleet overhung the dome (St. Paul's of course), rattled on it, and rolling westward became a radiant mountain-land, partly worthy of Victor's phrase: 'A range of Swiss Alps in air.'

"'With periwigs Louis Quatorze for peaks,' Colney added.

"And Fenellan improved on him. 'Or a magnified bench of Judges at the trial of your Caerulean Phryne.'"

It is, however, the Rev. Septimus Barmby who closes this contest of descriptive wit, "proclaiming that he had seen 'Chapters of Hebrew History in the grouping of clouds'." For wit, for copious reference, for oddly turned phrase, the passage is memorable. The images clash and quarrel with each other; yet out of their confusion comes a picture vivid and strong. Here Meredith's technique is abundantly justified by its effect.

Meredith, however, after forcing the potentialities of the language, was yet unsatisfied. He felt the need for linguistic invention to supplement his turn of phrase. Accordingly, he became a coiner of words; and it is this that allies him in one very essential point of his style with Peacock.

Before passing on to consider this interesting process in detail, it may be well to consider what Meredith himself has to say of his diction, the defense that he makes in its behalf. It is in *Sandra Belloni*, under cover of comment upon Tracy Runningbrook's novel, that Meredith gives discussion to the subject. Quite evidently he is thinking of his own practice; and the passage may be taken as a kind of apology.[5] "You say, 'He coins words;' and he certainly forces the phrase here and there, I must admit. The point to be considered is, whether fiction demands a perfectly smooth surface. Undoubtedly a scientific work does; and a philosophic treatise should. When we ask for facts simply, we feel the intrusion of a style. Of fiction it is part. In one case, the classical robe, in the other any mediaeval phantasy of clothing." Further he writes, "And more than this; our language is

---

[4] *One of Our Conquerors*, Vol. 17, Ch. IX, p. 87.
[5] *Sandra Belloni*, Vol. 3, Ch. VIII, p. 63.

not rich in subtleties for prose. A writer who is not servile and has insight must coin from his own mint. In poetry we are rich enough; but in prose also we owe everything to the license our poets have taken in the teeth of critics."[6] Apprehending, however, the chaos into which language would be thrown if every man essayed a personal style, Meredith adds a qualification to his advocacy of originality. "And, now you will be surprised to learn that, notwithstanding what I have said, I should still side with Mr. Runningbrook's fair critic, rather than with him. The reason is, that the necessity to write as he does is so great that a strong barrier—*a chevaux de frise* of pen points—must be raised against every newly minted word and hazardous coiner or we shall be innundated. If he can leap the barrier he and his goods must be admitted. So it has been with our greatest, so it must be with the rest of them." Evidently, from his persistent innovation, it was Meredith's assurance that he would be one of the happy few, the saved remnant of "the greatest."

Although Meredith, when he speaks of "coinage" and "newly minted words," is obviously thinking of his general free use of language; more particularly, he must have employed the terms also with the thought of specific word invention; the out-and-out creation of words from classic roots, to which he was somewhat habituated. It is in this trick that he shows a close alignment with Peacock, a following of the well-worn path which the elder man had taken.

Concerning Peacock's prose style it must be pointed out that he wrote, at choice, in two different manners. When he cared to, he wrote in a simple Anglo-Saxon style, notable both for its clarity and force. His novel *The Misfortunes of Elphin* contains, alike in the descriptive and expository passages, the most numerous and best examples of this honest English style. What, as an exposition of the Conservative point of view could be more effective than the burlesque speech put in the mouth of Seithenyn ap Seithenyn, Governor of the Royal Embankment. "Decay," said Seithenyn, "is one thing, and danger is another. Everything that is old must decay. That the embankment is old, I am free to con-

---

[6] *Sandra Belloni*, Vol. 3, Ch. VIII, p. 64.

fess; that it is somewhat rotten in parts, I will not altogether deny; that it is any the worse for that, I do most sturdily gainsay. It does its business well; it works well; it keeps the water out from the land, and it lets in the wine upon the High Commission of Embankment. Cup-bear, fill. Our ancestors were wiser than we: they built it in their wisdom; and if we should be so rash as to try to mend it, we should only mar it.'"[7] Here is English unadorned; the phrasing is precise, the principles of climax and antithesis are neatly employed, so that the effect of formal rhetoric is secured; but the words themselves are entirely unpretending. It is Peacock writing in his English manner.

This, however, is not the more usual manner of Peacock's writing. For the table-talk of his "phantasts" he employs the same careful rhetoric, but coupled with it is a vocabulary which often is as unusual and freakish as the opinions which the words express. Peacock as a coiner of words from Latin and Greek roots is not to be taken too seriously. Peacock's exotic words are not the works of necessity, but are a part of his whimsical humor. That he could have expressed himself with equal facility in a more commonplace diction is made clear by the specimens of a simpler style that he has left; moreover, his thought never exceeds the ready resources of the English tongue. Peacock's highly individual classical diction then is an affectation, a special sort of language which he gives to his scholars and "phantasts" as their appropriate property; the pedantic idiom of the learned and dogmatic. That Peacock liked to "dress-up" the language of his people in this way can scarcely be doubted; as an amateur classicist he apparently loved grubbing among ancient roots for the minting of new words, at once luminous and obscure. As a result of this penchant, Peacock's language tends, more or less, to be that of a coterie; it is an idiom full of humor, a joy to the initiated, but necessarily something of a mystery to those outside the pale of classical training.

To begin with, it must be said that Peacock does not always use his classical idiom with the purpose of startling; he has a classical jargon which he regularly employs for ordinary, pedes-

---

[7] *Misfortunes of Elphin*, Ch. II, p. 13.

trian purposes. For example, Peacock's people always "perlustrate"; never do they wander or walk abroad. Likewise, his people consistently "vaticinate"; never prophesy. In the same way, words such as "adhibit," "unconsentaneous," and "veridicous" appear, again and again, as habitual terms, until one becomes quite accustomed to them. Again one reads of "appetencies" and "prospiciencies" without any sense of humorous intention in the author; and adjectives abound (atrabilarious, autochthonal, conterminal, irremissible, pallescent) which seem more unusual then pretentious.

Peacock, more usually, however, is using his classical terms to secure an oracular tone for his speakers. When, for example, Mr. Portpipe, in *Melincourt*, pronounces, "Whisky is hepatic, phlogistic, and exanthematous; wine is the hierarchial and archepiscopal fluid,"[8] one understands that the imposing diction is part of the play of comedy. Likewise to call a drinking bout a "compotatory ceremonial";[9] an insulting epithet, "a dyslogistic term";[10] or to describe a hanged man as "funipendulous,"[11] is simply to raise a smile at the quaintness of the terms employed. It is in the pursuit of this sort of playful effect, that Peacock carries his diction far afield, sometimes to scarcely warrantable extremes. For example, Dr. Folliott does not beat the foot-pads who way-lay him; he "contunds" them.[12] Again, Dr. Folliott does not call his slanderer "defaming," but "inficete".[13] Sometimes, however, when the "big" word describes some simple action, or translates a familiar idiom, it is most effective. For instance when we are told of the little, timid friar, in *Maid Marion*, not that his words stuck in his throat, but that they "conglobated," the word is so effective in the image that it calls up that we could wish for no other.[14] In the same way the description of Dr. Folliott who "accinged" himself for the making of

---

[8] *Melincourt*, Ch. XVI, p. 122.
[9] *Ibid.*, Ch. XXVII, p. 207.
[10] *Crotchet Castle*, Ch. VIII, p. 218.
[11] *Misfortunes of Elphin*, Ch. VI, p. 47.
[12] *Crotchet Castle*, Ch. VIII, p. 218.
[13] *Ibid.*, Ch. VI, p. 199.
[14] *Maid Marian*, Ch. X, p. 79.

punch is equally felicitous in the picture it suggests.[15] The picture of Seithenyn, in *The Misfortunes of Elphin,* "oscillating like an inverted pendulum", then "straightening himself into perpendicularity," too is unforgettable for the same reason.[16]

More interesting still are those instances when Peacock invents his terminology. His description of the country gentry as an "agrestic kakistocracy" gives us his views of them in two words.[17] A mystical philosopher, a type for which Peacock had a real contempt, is termed a "mystagogue," obviously on the analogy to the demagogue whom Peacock feared and despised.[18] Most masterful of all, perhaps, is his description of Scythrop, the hero of *Nightmare Abbey,* as "jeremitaylorically pathetic.'"[19] At first glance the adjective looks like a bit of polysyllabic nonsense; but once the name of the great divine is apprehended in it, and the proper associations set in motion, it is seen as a stroke of insight, the inevitable word for the description of Scythrop's unhappy state.

That Meredith could imitate Peacock's diction perfectly, can be seen, at first hand, in his description of Dr. Middleton of *The Egoist,* and in Dr. Middleton's language. The character, it must be remembered, is based, at once, on Peacock's scholar-clergyman, and, as has been popularly asserted, on Peacock himself. In his description of Dr. Middleton "combining in himself piety and epicureanism, learning and gentlemanliness, with good room for each and a seat at one another's table," we catch the measured rhythm of Peacock's own descriptive formula.[20] Dr. Middleton's speech is even more reminiscent. To his daughter's question, "You wish to be near me, papa?" he replies, "Proximate— at a remove: communicable."[21] This, of course, is Peacock's very language; the perfect reproduction of his characters' talk. When the good doctor speaks of "the mysteries of erotic esotery," the echo rings clear.[22]

---

[15] *Crotchet Castle,* Ch. XVIII, p. 317.
[16] *Misfortunes of Elphin,* Ch. II, p. 11.
[17] *Ibid.,* Ch. VI, p. 47.
[18] *Crotchet Castle,* Ch. II, 372.
[19] *Nightmare Abbey,* Ch. VIII, p. 190.
[20] *The Egoist,* Vol. 13, Ch. XX, p. 225.
[21] *Ibid.,* Ch. VI, p. 62.
[22] *Ibid.,* Ch. XIX, p. 214.

That Meredith was master of his father-in-law's method and employed it, can be shown, however, from passages in other of his works, where he was not imitating any Peacockian character, but working independently. *Beauchamp's Career*, for example, is a novel full from first to last of recollections of Peacockian diction. Beauchamp, himself, is described as "pyro-cephalic" in true Peacockian fashion.[23] We are told further that thinking of England, dormant in political content, "he pummeled the obmutescent mass."[24] Cecelia, thinking of him, asks, "Why had he not sprung up in a radiant, aquiline ambition?"[25] The word "aquiline" is ambiguous, until one, as with Peacock, remembers the etymology, and reads "eagle-like" in its stead. Dr. Shrapnel counsels his young friend to remember that the public will "lapidate" (Why not stone?) men of their type.[26] At the close of the novel, the sounds made by Beauchamp in delirium are likened to those of a curate "galloping hippomanically through the Psalms."[27] Here, then, all the phenomena of the Peacockian classical jargon are reproduced; the sonorous classic term substituted for the humbler Anglo-Saxon; the term new-coined for its telling suggestiveness.

Although with Meredith a love of classic jargon never became a resource on which he placed first reliance, traces of it are to be found through his work. As late as the *Amazing Marriage*, there are vestiges of it; where he denominates Lord Fleetwood "deuteragonist,"[28] and calls his heroic women "prodigiosities,"[29] as in truth they are. It must be admitted this influence which descends from Peacock is of secondary importance; it is nowhere a great formative principle of Meredith's style. But when it does appear it is conspicuous, and its source is clear. As has been pointed out, Meredith's first effort was to make alive our native English by a novel handling of it; and to that effort the chief debt of his style is due. In that direction an obligation to Carlyle

---

[23] *Beauchamp's Career*, Vol. 11, Ch. XXXVIII, p. 304.
[24] *Ibid.*, Ch. IV, p. 40.
[25] *Ibid.*, Ch. XVIII, p. 175.
[26] *Ibid.*, Ch. XIX, p. 323.
[27] *Ibid.*, Ch. L, p. 570.
[28] *The Amazing Marriage*, Vol. 19, Ch. XX, p. 209.
[29] *Ibid.*, Ch. XXXVI, p. 377.

must be acknowledged, as the famous tribute to the "wind in the orchard style" in *Beauchamp's Career* clearly indicates. So far, however, as Meredith travelled beyond the bounds of our native English into the realm of classical invention, the debt is to Peacock. And here too, one difference must be pointed out. Peacock's use of a classical terminology was an integral part of his humor; with Meredith, except where he uses it in imitation of a Peacockian character, this is not so. In this respect Meredith follows Peacock in method, but not in spirit. Meredith's neologisms primarily are an earnest attempt to widen the range of the language; and, as such, fall in with his other innovations in diction. Accordingly, here as in so many other respects, although Meredith is following Peacock's method, he is doing so with a new intention; he is adapting rather than copying, and doing that with restraint.

BIBLIOGRAPHY

I. Editions

For the purposes of this thesis the following collected editions have been employed:

George Meredith, *The Works of George Meredith, Memorial Edition*, Constable, London, 1909–11; Scribner, New York, 1910–12.

(Note: The page references in the thesis apply equally to both the English and the American publications, since for both the pagination is the same.)

Thomas Love Peacock, the *Novels* and *Rhododaphne*, Macmillan, London, 1895–7, edited by George Saintsbury.

II Incidental Works

(not included in the collected editions)

George Meredith, *Up to Midnight*, Luce, Boston, 1913.

Thomas Love Peacock, *Letters to Edward Hookham and Percy Bysshe Shelley with Fragments of Unpublished Manuscripts*, Bibliographic Society, Boston, 1910. *The Four Ages of Poetry*, Blackwell, Oxford, 1923. *Calidore and Miscellanea*, edited by Richard Garnett, London, 1891.

BIOGRAPHIES AND MEMOIRS

GEORGE MEREDITH:

    Butcher, Lady Alice, *Memories of George Meredith*, New York, 1919.

    Ellis, S. M., *George Meredith, His Life and Friends in Relation to His Work*, London, 1920.

    Galland, René, *Les Cinquantes Premières Années*, Paris, 1923.

    Hardman, Sir William, *A Mid-Victorian Pepys, The Letters and Memoirs of Sir William Hardman*, London, 1923, edited by S. M. Ellis.

    Priestley, J. B., *George Meredith* in *English Men of Letters*, New York, 1926.

    Seccombe, Thomas, *George Meredith* in *the Dictionary of National Biography*.

    Selincourt, R. E., *The Life of George Meredith*, New York, 1929.

THOMAS LOVE PEACOCK:

    Cole, Sir Henry, *Thomas Love Peacock, Biographical Notes*, London, 1875.

    Freeman, A. M., *Thomas Love Peacock*, London, 1911.

    Priestley, J. B., *Thomas Love Peacock* in *English Men of Letters*, New York 1927.

    Van Doren, C., *The Life of Thomas Love Peacock*, New York, 1911.

CRITICISM

GEORGE MEREDITH:

    Bailey, E. J., *The Novels of George Meredith, A Study*, New York, 1907.

    Beach, J. W., *The Comic Spirit of George Meredith*, New York, 1911.

    Brownell, W. C., *Victorian Prose Masters*, New York, 1902.

    Chislett, W. J., *George Meredith, A Study and Appraisal*, New York, 1926.

    Crees, J. H. E., *George Meredith, A Study of His Works and Personality*, Oxford, 1918.

    Curle, R. H. P., *Aspects of George Meredith*, New York, 1908.

    Elton, O., *Modern Studies*, London, 1917.

    Frey, E., *Die Romane George Meredith's*, Winterthur, 1913.

    Gretton, M. S., *The Writings and Life of George Meredith*, London, 1926.

    Hammerton, J. A., *George Meredith, His Life and Art in Anecdote and Criticism*, Edinburgh, 1911.

    LeGallienne, R., *George Meredith, Some Characteristics*, London, 1890.

    Mackechnie, John, *George Meredith's Allegory, The Shaving of Shagpat, Interpreted*, London, 1905.

    Moffatt, James, *George Meredith, A Primer to the Novels*, London, 1909.

    Short, T. S., *On Some of the Characteristics of George Meredith's Prose Writings*, Birmingham, 1907.

    Photiades, C., *George Meredith, His Life, Genius and Teaching*, London, 1913.

    Torretta, L., *George Meredith, Romanziere, Poeta-Pensatore*, Naples, 1918.

    Trevelyan, G. M., *The Poetry and Philosophy of George Meredith*, London, 1907.

    Wolff, L., *George Meredith, Poète et Romancier*, Paris, 1927.

THOMAS LOVE PEACOCK:

    Saintsbury, George, *Introductions* to the several volumes of his edition of the novels, London, 1895–97.

    Young, A. B., *The Life and Novels of Thomas Love Peacock*, Norwich, 1904.

ARTICLES

Chislett, W. J., *Notes and Queries*, 11SX, Sept. 21, 1919.

Clodd, E., *George Meredith, Some Recollections*, *Fortnightly Review*, July, 1909.

"J. D. H.", *Notes and Queries*, 11S, VII, January 18, 1913.

Lee, J., *George Meredith's Literary Relations with Germany*, *Modern Language Review*, Oct., 1917.

Peacock, T. L., *Gastronomy and Civilization*, *Frazer's Magazine*, Dec., 1851.

Thomson, J., *Reviews of the Ordeal of Richard Feveral* and *The Egoist*, *Cope's Tobacco Plant*, Nos. 110, May 1879, and 118, Jan., 1880.

BIBLIOGRAPHIES

Forman, M. B., *A Bibliography of the Writings in Prose and Verse of George Meredith*, Edinburgh, 1922.
Forman, M. B., *Meredithiana*, Edinburgh, 1924.

CELTIC LITERATURE

Maclean, Magnus, *The Literature of the Celts*, London, 1906.
Skene, W. F., *The Four Ancient Books of Wales*, Edinburgh, 1868.